Plant
and
Animal Ways

by
Margaret Murphy

Standard Educational Corporation   Chicago 1990

Editing and Production by:

Creative Services Associates
Lynne Blanton

Design by:

De Pinto Graphic Design

Art by:

Masheris and Associates

Library of Congress Cataloging-in-Publication Data

Murphy, Margaret, 1929-
    Plant and animal ways / by Margaret Murphy.
        p.   cm. — (Child horizons)
    Rev. ed. of: Plant and animal ways / by Illa Podendorf. 1978
    Includes index.
    Summary: Discusses the characteristics of a representative sample
from the world's wide variety of animals and plants.
    ISBN 0-87392-114-3
    1. Animals—Juvenile literature.   2. Plants—Juvenile literature.
[1. Animals. 2. Plants.] I. Podendorf, Illa. Plant and animal
ways. II. Title
QL49.M87   1990   90-21885
574—dc20   CIP
                                                                      AC

To the Reader

It is fall, and in the sky flocks of birds are flying south. When winter is over and spring returns, the birds will come flying back again to their northern homes.

Birds don't have calendars to warn them of the approaching winter. They don't have maps or instruments to guide them. Yet they know when to fly south and how to get there. That is one of the wonders of nature.

Nature has many wonders. As we watch a beaver building its dam or ants scurrying in and out of an anthill or a spider weaving its web, we marvel at their knowledge and skill. The ways of the fish in the sea are marvelous, too. The chinook salmon swims from far out in the Pacific Ocean to the Columbia River to lay its eggs. It is a long and dangerous journey and yet each year thousands of salmon travel it.

The plant kingdom is full of wonders, too. There are plants so tiny that they can be seen only under a microscope. There are huge plants such as the California sequoia and redwood trees, which tower more than 300 feet (90 m) above the ground. Some of the sequoias are more than 3,000 years old. They were ancient trees when Columbus discovered America. They are among the oldest living things.

In this book, you will find information about these plants and animals and many others. And as you read, you will discover, too, how all plants and animals depend upon each other to survive.

Did you ever think how we depend on plants and animals? When people hunted and fished for their food and cut down trees to build their houses, they knew that without plants and animals they couldn't survive. Today we still depend on plants and animals for much of our food and shelter.

Plants and animals depend on us, too. They depend on us to help them survive in our changing world. We must make sure that people in the future will be able to see the wonders of nature that we enjoy now.

Plant and Animal Ways
Table of Contents

Plant and Animal Ways
Table of Contents

CLASSIFYING LIVING THINGS

How are things in the picture alike? How are they different from one another? Those are questions scientists ask when they classify the things on Earth. A rosebush doesn't look like a flock of chickens, but they are alike in a very important way: the roses and the chickens are alive.

What is a living thing? First, a living thing can grow. Second, it needs food and water to keep it living and growing. Third, it can produce more things like itself. Baby chicks eat bugs and grain, drink water, breathe air, and become roosters and hens. The hens lay eggs and more chicks hatch.

The rose grows from a tiny seed, becomes a flowering bush, grows larger each year, and produces seeds that will grow into other rosebushes. None of these things is true of a nonliving thing. A pile of sand is a nonliving thing. It doesn't need food, water, or air. It may get bigger, but only if more sand is added to it—it doesn't grow by itself. Look around you. Which of the things that you can see are living? Which are nonliving? Which aren't living now but came from something that lived?

There are many kinds of living things, but scientists divide all of them into groups, or *kingdoms*. One kingdom, whose members we see every day, is the *animal kingdom*. Usually it is easy to tell if something is an animal. Most animals move. They get food by eating plants or other animals. There are animals all around us: a pet dog, cat, or goldfish; an elephant in the zoo; cattle and pigs on the farms; butterflies and ants in the yard; birds in the air; people.

Another important kingdom is the *plant kingdom*. We know that most plants don't move, or at least not from place to place. Many plants are green. We know plants need good soil and water. Plants around us include tiny flowers in the grass and enormous trees in the forest.

There are three other kingdoms whose members may not be as familiar. For a long time, scientists put all living things in either the plant or the animal kingdom. Now, however, most scientists recognize five kingdoms: plant, animal, moneran, protist, and fungus.

The blue-green algae that we see on the top of a still pond is a *moneran*. So are the bacteria that live in our bodies or that cause disease. *Protists* are single-celled and some may cause diseases, such as malaria. Some monerans and protists are *microscopic*. This means you can see them only with the help of a microscope.

The *fungus kingdom* includes many living things we can see every day. Common fungi are mushrooms, mold, yeast, and mildew.

How do scientists decide which living things belong in each kingdom? They must examine each living thing and ask and answer questions about it. Then they find out ways in which things are alike. If two living creatures are alike in most important ways, they are in the same kingdom. Chickens and roses, as you have seen, are alike in some ways. But they are different in important ways, too. Chickens move around freely. They eat grain and lay eggs. Chickens also make noises that only other chickens may understand. Roses can't do any of these things. Chickens are animals; roses are plants.

ANIMALS

Backbones and Skeletons

Compare a fly with an eagle. They are alike in some ways. They move about. They must eat to live. Both of them fly. Flies and eagles are animals, but they are different in more ways than they are alike.

There are differences among animals, so scientists begin by dividing the animal kingdom into two large groups. In one group are animals with backbones. A backbone is made up of small bones fitted together, a little like beads on a string. These small bones are called *vertebrae*. Animals that have backbones are called *vertebrates*. An eagle is a vertebrate.

Animals that don't have backbones, and there are many of them, are called *invertebrates*. A fly is an invertebrate.

People have backbones so they are vertebrates. Horses, dogs, birds, fish, toads, and snakes are other common vertebrates. Some invertebrates that we may see are moths, butterflies, spiders, crayfish, and snails. Did you notice that the vertebrates are usually larger than the invertebrates? Why?

A vertebrate has other bones besides a backbone. These bones form an internal skeleton. The way a skeleton is shaped gives the body its shape. A fish has a shape different from that of a bird because its skeleton is shaped differently.

The skeleton of a vertebrate helps to protect the delicate organs, such as the heart and the brain, on the inside of the body. Like the steel beams and girders of a skyscraper, the bones of the skeleton support the body and all its parts.

The skeleton lets the body move, too. A jointed skeleton permits animals to walk, swim, fly, and crawl.

Invertebrates have no internal skeletons to support their bodies. Some invertebrates have no hard parts at all and some, such as sponges and barnacles, aren't able to move about when they are adults. When they are young, they fasten themselves to something and remain there for life. A barnacle, for example, might fasten itself to a rock or to the hull of a ship.

Other invertebrates have hard outer coverings that help them protect themselves and keep their shapes. Crabs, lobsters, crayfish, and shrimp are this kind of invertebrate. Did you ever wonder why the hard outer shell doesn't keep the animal from growing? If the covering on a crayfish gets too small, the animal splits it open and crawls out; soon a new covering forms. Snails and oysters make their shells larger in another way: they grow new rims on their shells.

Insects are the largest group of invertebrates. In fact, there are more kinds of insects in the world than all other kinds of animals put together. Some insects have hard outer coverings. Like the crayfish, they split open this covering and form a new one as they grow. Other insects don't have this protective hard cover. Measuring worms, green tomato worms, and little white grubs are examples.

There are many different kinds of insects, but there is one way in which all insects are alike. Every insect has six legs. When you see an animal with six legs, you can be sure it is an insect. Even the caterpillar, which will some day be an adult insect, has six true legs.

Another group of invertebrates has eight legs. Spiders and ticks belong to this group, called *arachnids.*

A scientist observing a meerkat

Asking the Right Questions

How do scientists find out about animals? They observe and ask questions. What kind of body does the animal have? Is it covered with fur, feathers, or a scaly skin? How does it move about? What does it eat? Are the babies born live or do they come from eggs? Does it look and act like another animal? Sometimes a great deal of observation is needed before an animal can be classified. Scientists divide all vertebrates into five groups. The first two groups are warm-blooded animals. *Warm-blooded* means the animal's temperature stays almost the same all the time. For example, the normal temperature of most humans is about 98.6 degrees Fahrenheit (37 degrees Celsius). Even if illness causes the temperature to rise or fall, it only changes a few degrees.

Many of the animals we know best are *mammals*. Mammals are warm-blooded. These animals have fur or hair and feed their babies milk from the mother's milk glands. Most mammals bear live babies.

If an animal has feathers, it is in another group: *birds*. Birds are also warm-blooded, but birds lay eggs from which the babies hatch.

All other vertebrates are cold-blooded. *Cold-blooded* means that the animal's temperature changes to closely match the temperature of the air or water in which it lives. There are three groups of cold-blooded vertebrates.

Reptiles are cold-blooded, have scales, and usually lay eggs. Lizards, snakes, alligators, and turtles are reptiles.

Amphibians, also cold-blooded, live part of their lives on land and part in the water. Frogs are amphibians.

Fish are cold-blooded vertebrates that breathe with gills rather than with lungs and live in the water. Most fish lay eggs, although a few give birth to their young.

The animal kingdom hasn't always been like it is today. Scientists believe that the first living things appeared on Earth more than three billion years ago. These were very simple amoeba-like creatures. Then gradually, more complex creatures developed. Probably the invertebrates were first, then fish, amphibians, reptiles, birds, and finally mammals.

How do scientists know this? They have pieced together this amazing story from evidence found in rocks. As millions of years passed, layer after layer of rock formed. Preserved in each layer are traces of the life that existed on Earth at the time the rock was formed. These traces, pressed into the rock, are called *fossils*.

After the first vertebrates appeared, there were so many fish that this period of time is called the Age of Fishes. Later, great swampy forests covered much of the world. During this time so many kinds of amphibians developed that the period is often called the Age of Amphibians. Next came the Age of Reptiles and then the Age of Mammals. Humans are mammals.

When a new type of animal appeared, did the old ones die out? Not always, but we do know some animals from the past no longer live anywhere on Earth. An animal that no longer exists is *extinct*. Perhaps

Tyrannosaurus, a dinosaur

the best-known extinct animals are the dinosaurs—animals that were the strongest force on Earth for millions of years. The name *dinosaur* comes from the Greek words that mean "monstrous lizard." Some dinosaurs were small, but others were enormous; Tyrannosaurus was 50 feet (15 m) long. Dinosaurs had very small brains, however, and for a long time some scientists thought this might have been at least part of the reason dinosaurs became extinct. There are many theories, but no one knows for certain why dinosaurs became extinct.

It took the dinosaurs thousands of years to disappear, but in the last 300 years, at least 300 kinds of vertebrates have become extinct. Most of these have died off because of the activities of their human neighbors.

MAMMALS

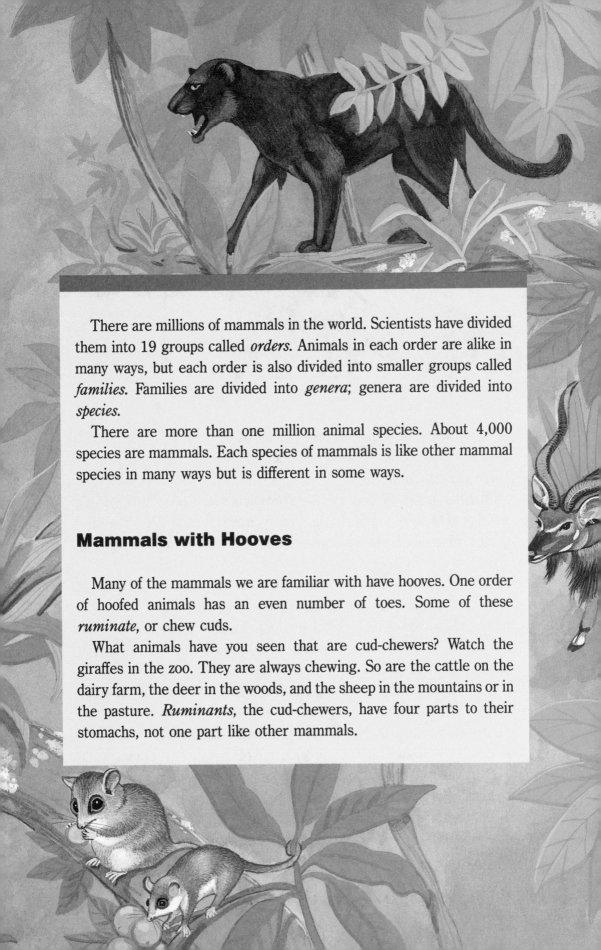

There are millions of mammals in the world. Scientists have divided them into 19 groups called *orders*. Animals in each order are alike in many ways, but each order is also divided into smaller groups called *families*. Families are divided into *genera*; genera are divided into *species*.

There are more than one million animal species. About 4,000 species are mammals. Each species of mammals is like other mammal species in many ways but is different in some ways.

Mammals with Hooves

Many of the mammals we are familiar with have hooves. One order of hoofed animals has an even number of toes. Some of these *ruminate*, or chew cuds.

What animals have you seen that are cud-chewers? Watch the giraffes in the zoo. They are always chewing. So are the cattle on the dairy farm, the deer in the woods, and the sheep in the mountains or in the pasture. *Ruminants*, the cud-chewers, have four parts to their stomachs, not one part like other mammals.

There are some even-toed hoofed animals that don't chew cuds. Pigs have two toes; so have camels, llamas, and hippopotamuses. None of these are cud-chewers.

Another order of hoofed animals includes all those with an odd number of toes. Tapirs are in this order; so are rhinoceroses. The most common family of odd-toed hoofed animals includes zebras, donkeys, and horses.

Millions of years ago a small four-footed animal, no larger than a fox, lived on the American continent. It had three toes on each of its hind feet and four toes on each of its front feet. When it walked it put its feet flat on the ground with every step. It roamed in herds and lived on plants.

This little creature was about 12 inches (30 cm) tall and it was much smaller and weaker than many of the other beasts that roamed the land at that time. But it was a very important animal. Its name was *eohippus*, the Dawn Horse, the ancestor of the modern horse.

Over the centuries, the tiny eohippus went through many changes and stages of development before it became the horse of today. In the diagram on this page, you can see some of the changes in this animal's size, shape, and way of walking. Scientists have studied the fossil

Eohippus, the Dawn Horse

remains in layers of rock. From this, they know some of this mammal's story, from eohippus to horse.

How and why did the little Dawn Horse change? We don't know all of the reasons, but we do know many of them. The horses didn't have claws or sharp teeth with which to defend themselves. When they were attacked by the huge meat-eating animals around them, they had to run for their lives.

They couldn't run very fast on their flat feet. For some reason, some began to run on their toes. These animals were faster and survived. Gradually, the little horses changed, or *evolved*.

Among some types of living things, those that are best fitted to live will survive, perhaps because they are swift or strong. Those that aren't fitted to find food or to escape enemies may not survive. Over hundreds or thousands of years these species may completely disappear. Records in the rocks show that the horse began to grow larger about the same time it started to use its toes. Its jaws and teeth grew stronger; its legs grew longer. As these changes took place, all of the horse's toes except one on each foot gradually disappeared. This toe is big and strong and is surrounded by a horny hoof, which is like a large hard toenail.

Belgian draft horses

As the horse developed, it spread to almost every part of the world, for horses can live in almost every climate. On the walls of caves in Europe there are ancient pictures of horses, drawn by the early people who lived in those caves.

The cave people hunted horses for meat. Later, horses were tamed and hunters rode horseback as they pursued other animals. Still later, horses were ridden into battle by soldiers. You have probably seen pictures of European knights in the Middle Ages, dressed in heavy armor and riding huge, powerful horses. When we compare those horses with the tiny eohippus, we can see the result of evolution over the centuries. Descendants of those war horses were later used to pull plows and heavy carts. This type of horse is called a draft horse. There are many kinds of draft horses. Some of the best-known are Belgian, Percheron, Shire, and Clydesdale.

Although the little Dawn Horse had lived first on the American continent, horses had disappeared from that continent before people came. The first horses used by Indians were brought to the continent by soldiers and explorers who came from Spain in the early 1500s.

Some of these horses ran away. Grassy plains and clear streams provided food and water for them. Bands of wild horses spread across the continent. Descendants of the Spanish horses still live in a few parts of North America today. They are called mustangs.

As the Indians became more familiar with horses, they learned to capture and tame them. They soon came to depend on the swift animals to help them hunt.

In many parts of the world, horses were the chief form of transportation. Many people rode horses. Horses pulled carriages and wagons.

In the 1700s, James Watt invented a new type of steam engine. When he began to sell the engines, he wanted to tell buyers just how powerful each engine was. Watt figured out how much work a horse could do; then he told the buyer how many horses would be needed to do the work of the engine. A six-horsepower engine could do what six horses could do. Even today, engines are measured in horsepower, but today one horsepower is the power needed to lift 33,000 pounds one foot in one minute. That is actually about 1½ times the power an ordinary horse can exert. (The metric unit corresponding to horsepower is the watt. One horsepower equals 745.7 watts.)

In the 1800s, after the gasoline engine was invented, making cars and trucks possible, horses began to be used less often for transportation. However, in some areas they are still important for work and transport. Herders of cattle and sheep may ride horseback. A special horse was developed for this purpose. It is called a quarter horse because it can run swiftly for about a quarter of a mile (two fifths of a kilometer). The quarter horse is surefooted and can start, turn, and stop at the rider's slightest signal.

In many places, people still hunt on horseback. They like to watch horse races and horse shows and polo games. Horses are widely used by people who ride for pleasure. Even in large cities, there are often riding paths for riders and their horses. Stables may provide areas for riding and jumping.

Race horses are called Thoroughbreds. All Thoroughbreds are descendants of three famous horses from Arabia. They were brought to Europe in the 1700s. Many hunting horses and polo horses also have Arabian blood.

Two popular horses for pleasure riding are the American Saddle Horse and the Tennessee Walking Horse. Both are friendly and gentle. These were developed by American plantation owners who wanted a gentle horse that would be comfortable to ride over long distances.

Another popular riding horse is the Morgan. It is a small horse, but bold and strong, and is especially good for riding on rough trails. All

Morgan horses are descended from a horse owned by an American schoolteacher in the 1800s.

There are many, many kinds of horses. A small horse that will grow no more than 58 inches (147 cm) high is called a pony. A favorite pony is the Shetland from the Shetland Islands. It is a gentle, friendly animal, not much bigger than a large dog.

Other members of the horse family are the zebra, the donkey, and the mule. Donkeys, like horses, have been tamed, or *domesticated*, in many parts of the world. Large donkeys and tiny ones called burros are sometimes ridden but are more often used as pack animals. Donkeys are very strong and surefooted. They are often used on mountain trails.

Zebras aren't tame. These beautiful striped creatures live in Africa, in the grasslands where their stripes help them to blend in with their surroundings. They are fast and quick to respond to danger.

A mule is a cross between a female horse and a male donkey. Known for its endurance, strength, surefootedness, and ability to work in harsh conditions, the mule was a popular work animal throughout history and around the world.

There is a special vocabulary that people use when discussing members of the horse family. An adult female horse is a mare and a young female is a filly. An adult male horse is a stallion and a young male is a colt. A baby horse, male or female, is called a foal.

Special words are also used to describe a horse's appearance. Some horses have coats of solid colors such as black, chestnut, bay, white, gray, or golden palomino. Others have coats of mixed colors. Indian ponies often had brown or white spots. These were called "paint" ponies, or pintos.

Horses are usually measured in *hands*. A hand is four inches (10 cm). A horse's height is measured from the ground to its withers, the ridge between the shoulder bones.

Horses are found today in almost all parts of the world, because people have brought them to most areas where they were not already present. There are many famous horses in history and in fiction.

Why are horses so important? Think of the ways human beings changed how they lived when they found and tamed horses.

Fox

Gerald & Buff Corsi/**TOM STACK & ASSOCIATES**

Wolf

Gary Milburn/**TOM STACK & ASSOCIATES**

Mammals With Claws

Another order of mammals is a group called *carnivores,* or meat-eaters. These animals have toes with claws. Some of them have claws that can be pulled in, or *retracted.* Two of the most common house pets are carnivores—one has retractable claws and the other has unretractable claws. Do you know what they are?

The meat-eaters with unretractable claws include many familiar animals: dogs, wolves, jackals, and foxes are one type; bears are another type; raccoons and pandas are a third type of carnivore with unretractable claws; weasels, skunks, and otters form a fourth group. These animals all have well-defined snouts as well as unretractable claws.

Thousands of years ago, all dogs were wild. In different parts of the world, wolves, dingos, coyotes, jackals, and other wild dogs lived mostly on animals they killed or that had been killed by others. These wild dogs usually lived in packs. Each pack had a leader and every animal had a place and role in the pack.

Eventually, people began to tame young wild dogs. They taught the dogs to use their hunting instincts to help the people find game. They could also teach the dogs to use their protective instincts to guard or herd animals.

Like their wild relatives, modern dogs have the sharp, pointed teeth of many meat-eating mammals and they still have the keen senses that made them good hunters. Dogs have eyes that are quick to see any movement. They can see some colors, though not as many as humans can. Dogs can hear sounds we can't hear and most of them have an unusually keen sense of smell. Dogs have five toes on their front paws and four on their hind paws. Each toe has a sharp claw.

Because dogs are intelligent and because they lived in packs and followed leaders, they were easier to tame than some other animals. A dog will follow its human owner much as a wild dog will follow a pack leader, and dogs like to be with other dogs or with people.

The first tamed dogs were probably used as watch dogs and hunting dogs, as they are today. There are many modern hunting breeds, each with its own hunting style. Pointers and setters can catch the scent of a bird from a distance. They will stand and point at the bird, or indicate its position, until the hunter sees it. Retrievers will go after a bird that has been shot and bring it back. Some work best on land, others in water. Beagles and foxhounds will follow the scent of an animal for a long way and guide the hunter to the animal. Some dogs will chase an animal up a tree, then stay under the tree until the hunter arrives. Terriers will dig game out of underground holes.

Almost any dog will show some signs of its ability to hunt—a skill that is left over from the days when all dogs were wild and had to find food. Police today often use the hunting instinct of bloodhounds to track people. Because these dogs have an unusually keen sense of smell, they can follow a person's scent. Other dogs with keen smell can be trained to sniff out illegal drugs being smuggled into a country.

Another early use of dogs probably was for herding. Wolves would, by instinct, circle a herd of animals before separating one from the herd and killing it. The same instinct led the tame dogs to circle herds and drive the animals together, helping the shepherd who had to keep a large flock of sheep in one place. When a herd of cows is moving to the barn to be milked, a good herd dog will nip at the heels of any cow that is wandering away from the herd.

Dogs are often trained to do important work for people. Some dogs are trained to act as guide dogs for people who are blind. A guide dog wears a harness with a stiff leash. The dog learns to follow directions such as "left" or "right" and to watch for obstacles, for steps, and for traffic.

A guide dog is also taught to disobey a command if it is going to place the person it is guiding in danger. For example, if the dog is told to start across a busy street, it won't obey until traffic clears.

The training of a guide dog takes about four months. The person who will work with the dog joins in for part of the training period. Not all dogs make good guide dogs. German shepherds are used most frequently.

Dogs are also trained to help people who are hearing-impaired. These dogs are trained to listen for doorbells, telephones, and sirens, and to alert their owners to the sounds.

In some places, dogs are used to help the police and to guard property. In wars, dogs have been used to carry messages and to walk with a soldier on guard duty.

For centuries, people who lived in Alaska, Siberia, and other places in the far north have trained teams of dogs to pull sleds. Walking and using dogsleds were the only means of transportation in these areas. While snowmobiles have taken the place of these dogs in many places, the dogs are still used occasionally and dogsled racing has become a popular sport.

Did dogs always look like they do today? Probably not. As dogs were used for special kinds of work, they were bred to keep the qualities that made them successful. For example, two dogs that were especially fast would have puppies that were very fast. Two dogs that had long soft hair would have puppies with long soft hair. Some of the breeds of dogs we see today have been bred because someone liked one or two characteristics the dog had. These carefully bred dogs are raised by breeders and are entered in dog shows all over the world. In these shows, dogs are judged on appearance and obedience and are sometimes entered in contests to show hunting ability. The best dog of each breed is given a blue ribbon. These champions are worth a lot of money to the dog breeder. Raising dogs is an important business today.

None of the other carnivores with unretractable claws have been domesticated in the way dogs have. Bears are found in most parts of the world and chiefly in the wild. Polar bears, black and brown bears, and sun bears are a few common bears. Pandas, another carnivore, live in the wild. Small carnivores, such as skunks and raccoons, are occasionally tamed and they adapt easily to life near humans, but most are wild animals.

Among carnivores with retractable claws, cats are the most common and probably the most familiar. If you watch a playful kitten stalk a piece of yarn, pounce on a ball, or lie lazily in the sun, you will begin to understand this family of carnivores.

Although a pet cat is clearly quite different from a tiger or a leopard, it is also much like them. An important likeness that puts them in the

Panda

Skunk

same family is their feet. Cats have five toes on each front foot and four on each hind foot. These toes have very sharp, retractable claws. Keeping the claws retracted keeps them strong and sharp. Some cats use these claws to help them climb. Behind the toes and under the balls of a cat's feet are soft cushions which make it easy for the cat to move quietly. All cats also use these soft paws for cleaning or grooming. They lick their paws and rub their faces until they are clean.

Another way that all cats are alike is in their choice of food. Cats, like dogs, are carnivores. This means that they are hunters. Cats, unlike dogs, are night hunters. Their eyesight is very keen in the dark, and their whiskers help them feel objects in the dark.

One of the most powerful members of the cat family is the lion. A lion is a very large cat; it sometimes grows to be nearly four feet (1.2 m) tall from its paws to its shoulder and nine feet (2.7 m) long from the tip of its nose to the end of its tail. Because of its large size, the lion is a powerful hunter, with little to fear from other animals. There are very few animals that a lion will not attack. A full-grown elephant, a rhinoceros, and a hippopotamus are among the animals that are safe from lions.

Cheetah

John Shaw/**TOM STA**
& ASSOCIAT

Lion

Mark Newman/**TOM STACK & ASSOCIATES**

Like all mammals, young lions depend upon their mothers' milk for their first food. Lions live in groups called *prides,* and the young are carefully watched by both parents. If a female lion feels her cubs are threatened, she may move them, carefully carrying them in her jaws. Lion cubs need care until they are about two years old. At that time, they are able to hunt and can capture food for themselves.

There are wild cats in most parts of the world: cheetahs, leopards, tigers, cougars, and bobcats, for example. You know that dogs were domesticated because they could help people hunt and herd their animals. Why were cats domesticated? Most domestic cats are just pets. Although in some places cheetahs were trained to hunt deer, cats have almost never been used to help people hunt. Cats, though, do hunt for themselves and are often kept to control rats and mice.

Two other mammals that are carnivores with retractable claws are civets, catlike animals that live in central Africa, and hyenas. Hyenas are wild, look a little like dogs, and have a howl that sounds like a wild, loud laugh.

Gorilla

Marmoset

Joe McDonald/TOM STACK & ASSOCIATES

Chimpanzee

Mammals with Hands

The order of mammals called *primates* is divided into two groups: mammals with longer snouts, such as tree shrews and lemurs, and those with short snouts or flatter faces. This second group includes marmosets, New World monkeys, baboons, Old World monkeys, and the tailless monkeys we call apes: gibbons, gorillas, chimpanzees, and orangutans. People are also primates.

While we may see monkeys and their relatives in zoos everywhere today, they were originally found in only a few parts of the world. All primates, except people, are native to Africa, southern Asia, or Central and South America.

Many monkeys live in families or groups of families. They have leaders and each monkey learns the way to behave toward leaders and toward one another. Monkeys spend much time caring for one another. A new baby monkey will be held by all the female monkeys. Monkeys groom one another. This means they search through other monkeys' fur, removing dry skin or bugs. Most monkeys live in trees, and some of them rarely come down to the ground. They have become very skillful at swinging long distances from branch to branch and tree to tree, using their hands to hold on. A New World monkey has additional help as it swings along; its tail is long and so strong that the monkey can loop it around a branch and hang by its tail.

Monkeys have two hands and two feet. On each hand is a thumb. This thumb enables monkeys to hold onto branches with ease, grab food, and groom one another.

Monkeys are many colors; some even display bright shades of blue or red. Brown is most common, however. Most monkeys are quite small. Their size helps them to live easily in the high trees. Since most monkeys are natives of hot climates, they are generally active in the morning and evening, using the hot afternoon for quiet activities like eating.

Monkeys have been tamed and kept as pets for thousands of years. Some types of monkeys are more popular than others. Marmosets are only about eight inches (20 cm) tall and have soft, fluffy fur. The squirrel monkey has a pleasant disposition and loves to be held and petted. Circuses often use rhesus monkeys. These animals are easy to raise and can stand cold weather better than other monkeys.

A monkey relative that doesn't live in trees is the baboon. It lives on the ground among rocks and hills. It runs swiftly on all four legs. Baboons live in herds, feeding together on fruits, roots, birds' eggs, and insects. Baboons have large cheek pouches which they fill with food before they swallow. Baboons can be dangerous to humans if they feel threatened. They are native to Africa and Arabia.

Tailless primates, apes, are larger than monkeys. A full-grown gorilla in the African tropical rain forest may be six feet (1.8 m) tall and weigh over 400 pounds (180 kg). Chimpanzees, which also live in Africa, are not as large as gorillas, but they are much bigger than monkeys. Chimps are considered the most intelligent of all the apes. They have been trained to follow complicated directions and to communicate by pushing buttons or selecting cards with words on them. A chimpanzee named Enos was sent into space at the beginning of the United States' space program to test how space and weightlessness might affect the performance of human astronauts.

Mouse

Gnawing Mammals

The most common mammals in the world are animals that *gnaw*, that is, bite persistently. These mammals are called *rodents*. No matter where we live, we can see rodents.

Most rodents, such as rats, mice, squirrels, and lemmings, are small. A few, such as the mountain beaver, are a little larger. The capybara, found in Brazil, is the largest rodent—about the size of a pig. Rodents can do enormous damage. In fact, the word *mouse*, which comes from an ancient language called Sanskrit, means "thief." Rodents have always been considered thieves and pests. A *pest* is an animal that is either too abundant or in the wrong place. Most of the time, pests are just annoying, but they can cause great economic damage. All continents except Antarctica have native rodents, and most of them also have rodents that have been brought in by people who came from other lands. For example, rats have traveled on ships ever since big sailing vessels began crossing the seas. When a ship landed on a new continent or island, its cargo was unloaded and some of the rats also

Squirrel

left and made their home in the new land. Still other rodents have been introduced as pets by settlers in foreign lands. An example is the Mongolian gerbil, which is sold as a pet in many countries.

Squirrels, chipmunks, and marmots are different from mice and rats, but they are also rodents. Different types of these small mammals are native to North America, Europe, Asia, and parts of South America and Africa. There are more than 200 varieties of squirrels, chipmunks, and marmots. Most are red, gray, or black. In tropical countries and in parts of Asia, squirrels may be brilliant colors. There are squirrels with tufted ears and squirrels that jump from branches and glide so far that they are called "flying squirrels."

Squirrels eat a variety of food, mostly seeds and grains. They will also crack and eat nuts. Squirrels have long sharp teeth in front, two in each jaw. They use these teeth to gnaw holes in the hard shells of nuts so they can get to the soft part inside. Squirrels often bury nuts and later dig them up. The squirrels don't remember where they buried each nut: a keen sense of smell helps them to find the buried food.

Squirrels that live in changeable climates usually have two homes: a nest on a branch is a summer home, and a hole in a tree provides more shelter in storms or in cold weather.

Most members of the squirrel family live in trees, but some, such as the chipmunk, live on the ground. Other ground squirrels are the gopher, the marmot, and the prairie dog.

Beaver lodge

Beaver

Another rodent, the beaver, is native to North America and to central Europe. Beavers are hard-working animals. Sometimes, when you're working very hard, you may hear someone say, "You're as busy as a beaver." If you have ever watched a beaver, you will understand why this comparison is made.

A full-grown beaver is about four feet (1.2 m) long from the tip of its nose to the end of its tail. It may weigh up to 66 pounds (30 kg). Yet an animal this small will cut down a tree, remove the branches, cut the tree into lengths it can move, and take them into the river or pond where it is building its home.

Beavers work early in the morning or during the night to be safe from enemies. The beaver leaves its home, or *lodge*, in a pond or on the bank of a stream. It selects a tree and begins gnawing at the trunk, close to the bottom. Beavers have two sharp upper teeth which bite into the hard wood, and two sharp lower teeth which cut away wood pieces. Chip by chip, the tree is gnawed until there is a deep groove all around the trunk. When enough cuts have been made, the tree begins to fall. The beaver slaps the ground with its wide, flat tail, making a loud warning noise so all the other beavers will move away from the falling tree.

When the tree is down, the beaver gnaws off the branches and cuts the tree into lengths that it can move. Both branches and logs are important. They will be used to build a new lodge or to repair the old one, which is always in need of a patch or an addition. The bark is used for food. Beavers also eat tree roots, which they dig out of the ground using the long sharp claws on their front paws.

A beaver lodge looks like a huge heap of branches and mud, but it is actually a carefully built structure. Each branch and stick is placed exactly to support the dome-shaped roof. Walls may be three feet (0.9 m) thick. When logs and sticks are in place, the beaver holds mud against its body and carries it to the lodge. It then plasters the mud firmly over the branches and sticks.

A beaver lodge is a room about seven feet (2.1 m) across and 18 inches (46 cm) high. It is above the water level and has an air hole in the roof. The only entrance to the lodge is through a tunnel under the water. Some beavers dig a second room under the top room and use it as a storehouse for branches and twigs. Other beavers store a pile of branches underwater near the tunnel entrance. They stick the branches firmly in the bottom of the stream or pond and sometimes anchor them with stones so the branches can't float away. All through autumn the beavers gather branches and twigs for their storehouse so that when winter comes they will have plenty to eat.

Sometimes a pair of beavers builds a lodge and lives in it alone, but most beavers live together in a group, or *colony*. If there are several families in a pond, they all work together to fill the storehouses and they all share the food.

Beavers may also work together to build dams. When the water in a stream or pond is too shallow for a beaver lodge, the animals build a strong wall of logs and sticks and weight it with stones and mud. This dam holds the water back and makes it rise. The beavers will build their dam higher and higher until the water is just deep enough for their lodges.

All beavers help to keep the dam strong. If it breaks, they quickly repair it. Sometimes fairly large logs are needed for the dam. If there aren't enough trees near the edge of the pond, the beavers may dig a canal about a yard (0.9 m) wide back into the woods. Then they can float logs out to the pond.

The entrance to a beaver lodge is always underwater. This is a protection from enemies. Wolverines, for example, are enemies of the beaver. When a beaver sees a wolverine, it gives the danger signal by slapping the water with its tail. Then it swims to its lodge. The wolverine can't swim underwater, so it can't follow. A beaver can swim underwater for a half mile (0.8 km) and hold its breath for 15 minutes if it needs to. Beavers' eyes are protected underwater by a transparent inner eyelid. This lid also protects against scratches from branches and wood chips when the beaver is grawing at a tree.

In the lodge, the beaver babies, called *kittens*, are born. The kittens, usually two to six each year, live on their mother's milk until they are about six weeks old. They follow their mother about, and they see her stripping bark from a tree to eat. When they are old enough, they begin to feed in this way.

Beavers must learn from their parents how to find food, but they don't need to learn how to swim. Beavers are more at home in water than on land from the time they can move around. They have webs of skin between the toes on their back feet and broad, flat tails that help them to balance and change direction. Young beavers live with their parents for about two years. They play a lot, but they also help with the constant work of finding food and repairing the lodge. When a beaver is old enough and finds a mate, it leaves home and begins to build its own lodge. Sometimes a beaver family will find that its food supply has disappeared or that too many enemies have moved into the area. Then they will move to a better place and build a new lodge.

Rabbits and Hares

Another order of small mammals includes rabbits and hares. Like rodents, these animals are often considered to be pests. They are native to both American continents and to Europe, Africa, and Asia. Rabbits were introduced into Australia by European settlers. There, where the rabbits had no natural enemies, they caused tremendous destruction. In other places, natural enemies such as foxes and owls usually keep the rabbit population under control. There is little difference between rabbits and hares, although hares are often larger.

The average life span of a wild rabbit is less than one year. Since each pair of rabbits may have four or five young four or five times a year, however, there are usually a lot of rabbits around.

Rabbits and hares are different from most mammals in that they don't walk or run; they jump. Their hind legs are extremely strong and each leap can carry them a great distance. Rabbits and hares also have long ears which are sensitive to the slightest sound. A rabbit can move one ear at a time, turning it to catch every noise. A rabbit also has a keen sense of smell, and because its eyes are positioned on the sides of its head, it can see in a wide angle.

Domestic rabbits

Holland Lop

Runk/Schoenberger from Grant Heilman

English Angora

Runk/Schoenberger from Grant Heilman

Rabbits and hares live in extremely cold climates and in hot deserts, but the animal that lives in the cold is different in some ways from the one that lives where it is hot. One difference can be seen in the rabbit's ears. Animals living in hot places have very long ears, since the surfaces of these body parts allow heat to escape. Some rabbits that live in snowy climates change fur color to match the surrounding land.

Most rabbits and hares are *nocturnal*. This means they sleep during the day and eat at night. Rabbits build nests in the ground or under bushes. European rabbits often live in complex systems of burrows and passageways called *warrens*. Many rabbit families will share each warren.

Rabbits and hares may be pests, but they are also kept for food, for hair, or as pets. Like dogs, rabbits have been bred so that today there are many types, each with a special characteristic. Some rabbits, for example, have long fine hair which is used for yarn. Others are very large, or have floppy ears, or produce good meat. Domestic rabbits are gentle and make good pets, but wild rabbits usually can't be tamed.

Insect-eating Mammals

Insectivores are mammals that eat insects. One member of this order is the mole, which lives underground in North America and across southern Europe and southeastern Asia.

Many people have never seen a mole because the small mammal spends most of its time underground. When the ground is dry, the mole works well below the surface of the soil because the earthworms and insects on which it feeds go down to find moisture. If the ground is wet, the mole burrows just below the surface of the soil. Then it leaves ridges on the grass or across the field. People often consider the mole a pest because it burrows under the grass and spoils the appearance of a smooth, green lawn, but moles are helpful because they eat many harmful insects.

A mole is only about five to eight inches (13-20 cm) long. It has small eyes and is almost blind. Since it lives mostly underground, the mole has no need for keen sight. Its hearing is also poor and it has no external ears, but a mole's sense of smell is good.

The mole is built for digging. It has a wedge-shaped head, a pointed nose, and forelegs which turn out and have long sharp nails on the toes. Even the mole's fur helps it to dig more efficiently. The hairs are laid so close together that dirt can't get into the fur. Mole fur is extremely soft and is a beautiful color.

Baby moles are born in a nest of roots and grasses in one of the underground burrows. They will stay with their mother for about five weeks until they are able to dig for their own food.

Moles are small but fierce. A person who picks up a mole would be making a serious mistake, and moles may attack humans or animals who threaten them. They will even attack their much larger enemy, the weasel.

Mammals That Fly

What small mammal flies like a bird and squeaks like a mouse? A bat! Bats have wings but no feathers. Bats can be up to 15 inches (38 cm) long. Most bats feed on insects which they catch in the air. There are so many bats in the world that if you were to line up all the mammals from all of the continents, every fourth animal would be a bat.

One reason that bats are so common is that they have filled a place held by no other animal. They are the only creatures that fly swiftly and freely at night. Bats aren't blind, but they don't see well and depend on a kind of radar. As bats fly, they cry out in a high pitch. Although the sound isn't in the range humans can hear, the bats' ears detect the sound very well. If anything is in the way, the sound echoes back from the object and the bats will avoid the object.

Another reason that bats are everywhere is their *adaptability*. This means they can change their habits to suit the places they live. For example, before humans settled in an area, bats lived in the wild—in caves or trees or cliffs. Then people moved in and most wild creatures moved away. But the bats remained, finding new places to live under eaves of roofs or in barns or attics.

Bats have fingers as long as their bodies. A thin fold of skin stretches from finger to finger, to the arm and body, and to the hind leg and tail. This thin skin forms a wing. A bat can dart about, changing direction rapidly. It has a perfect sense of control in flying and will almost never run into anything. During one night, a bat will find and eat about half of its weight in insects while flying in the dark.

Bats sleep through the day, hanging by their hind toes from a branch or ledge. One of the bat's claws is almost like a thumb; it can close over a branch much as a human hand would.

A mother bat usually has one or two babies at a time. Like all mammals, the babies drink their mother's milk until they are old enough to find food for themselves.

The Largest Land Mammal

Long ago, there were elephants on every continent except Australia and Antarctica. Today these unusual animals live wild only in Africa and India, and their survival in these places is also threatened.

The elephant is an amazing animal. It is enormous, but it is not carnivorous. It is *herbivorous*, living on grass and tree branches. Its feet are immense, but it can move almost soundlessly. It has a thick skin, but it shivers when the weather gets a little cool. It has two enormous front teeth, but it can't use them for biting. These powerful teeth, or *tusks,* can save the elephant when it fights an enemy but may cause its death because ivory tusks can be sold for a lot of money.

The elephant is the only mammal in its order. There is no other animal like it. Perhaps its strangest feature is its trunk, which is both a nose and an upper lip. The elephant uses its trunk to gather food, sometimes from the ground and sometimes from high on a tree. It can use its trunk to tear a huge limb from a tree or to pick up a tiny nut from the ground. The tip of the elephant's trunk can work almost like fingers when it wants to pick up a small object. The elephant's trunk can pick up cooling dust to spurt over its back and can fill with water to spray on its hot skin. The elephant uses its trunk like a cat uses its whiskers, to test for safety. An elephant will probe the ground with its trunk if it thinks it may be dangerous to take another step. Like most animals, the elephant will sniff the air for strange or dangerous scents. When an elephant swims, it may use its trunk like a diver would use an air tube, submerging except for the tip of the trunk.

Without its trunk an elephant would starve. Why? An elephant's legs are long, but its neck is short. A trunkless elephant would find it difficult to get food or water.

The word *trunk* as a name for the elephant's nose comes from a French word that means "trumpet," referring to the noise the elephant makes. The scientific name for the nose is *proboscis.*

There are two kinds of elephants, the African and the Indian. The African elephant is found in the warmest parts of Africa, while the Indian elephant is found in southern Asia and on some islands near the coast of Asia.

A herd of African elephants

The African elephant is the larger animal. Its trunk is wrinkled. Its immense ears hang over its shoulders and almost meet at the back of its head. The Indian elephant has a smoother trunk and smaller ears. Both elephants have skin that hangs in wrinkles and folds down their huge bodies and legs. Even young elephants have wrinkled skins.

An elephant will often travel a long way for water. Then it drinks as much as possible, storing the water in its stomach until it is needed. The elephant's teeth are good grinders. As they wear down, they move forward in the jaw and fall out. New teeth grow in to take their places. Elephants may have as many as six sets of teeth in a lifetime of fifty years.

Although elephants aren't carnivorous, they are so huge and powerful that other animals are careful not to make them angry. Even the fiercest wild animal rarely attacks a grown elephant.

An adult male elephant is called a bull, an adult female is a cow and a baby elephant is a calf. Elephants mate for life. They live and travel in herds, staying in the same group for many years. There are usually from 20 to 40 elephants in a herd, although there may be more. Each herd has a leader, and usually the elephants live peacefully together. The herd travels slowly as it searches for sources of food and water. The oldest and youngest elephants can keep up with the group. If a baby elephant is born while a herd is on the move to new grounds, the mother and baby set the pace. When the baby tires, the herd stops and waits for it to rest. When a river must be crossed, the mother holds her baby with her trunk. No land mammal is a better swimmer than an elephant.

When a baby elephant is born, it is about 2½ feet (0.75 m) tall and may weigh nearly 200 pounds (90 kg). Its skin is soft, wrinkled, and covered with soft hair. The baby is quite helpless and feeds on its mother's milk. Its trunk is still short and weak and is of little use. Gradually the baby learns to use its trunk.

Elephants grow slowly. A baby is protected by its mother until it is four or five years old. It won't be really grown up until it is about 13 years old.

Elephants move about mostly at night and sleep standing up during the day. Their big feet and pillarlike legs help them keep their balance so they can rest while standing up.

In spite of their enormous size, elephants have been domesticated for centuries. They have been used to move heavy objects and to carry people on their backs. In some places, they are still used to do heavy work.

A Sea-going Mammal

We know that many of the land mammals move from place to place to search for food or to escape cold weather. But they are limited in their movement, for eventually they will reach the ocean and have to stop. For this reason, land animals that can't fly must remain on one continent. But the largest of all mammals has no such limits. Whales have the freedom to swim through all the oceans of the world. Whales travel from one ocean to another, making long journeys. Some travel alone, but many move in groups. Some whales use warmer waters for breeding and raising young, but in the summer they move to cold waters and feed on a kind of sea animal called krill.

Whales may be 10 times the size of the largest land mammal, the elephant. Even a baby whale may outweigh a grown elephant. Although they live in oceans, whales are mammals, producing live young that feed in their early months on their mothers' milk.

Whales' bodies are shaped like fishes' bodies. They are streamlined so they meet with less resistance from the water. Whales swim with their tails and their front legs, or flippers, just as fish swim with their tails and fins. Some whales even have fins on their backs—but whales aren't fish.

Fish breathe through gills, taking in oxygen from the water. Whales have lungs, just like tigers and elephants, apes and people, and they must breathe air. A whale may stay underwater for a long time, but then it will surface, blow the air out of its lungs, and take in fresh air. When the air pushes out of a whale's lungs, water above it is pushed out, too, making a spout that may rise 15 feet (4.5 m) high, like a fountain. Baby whales can swim when they are born. They follow their mothers through the water almost immediately. A baby whale is called a calf.

Under the gray or black skin of whales is a thick layer of fat which protects the animals from the cold water. It also protects them from the bites of other animals and from the heavy pressure of the water when they swim deep beneath the surface. This fat may be as much as two feet (0.6 m) thick!

A gray whale blowing

Grant Heilman

Humpback whale

There are many kinds of whales. Some have plates of bone which hang from the roofs of their mouths. These plates, fringed on the edges, act as strainers and the whale's open mouth strains out large objects but takes in small animals such as crabs and small fish. When its mouth is full, the whale raises its huge tongue and squeezes the water from the plants and animals it has caught. Then the food is swallowed down a tube, or gullet, which leads to the stomach.

Whales which have teeth have bigger throats. The teeth may be a foot (30 cm) long and 10 inches (25 cm) around. Some kinds of whales have both upper and lower teeth, but others have teeth only on the lower jaws. These toothed whales eat bigger animals, such as giant squids and penguins.

The largest of all animals, on land or in the sea, are the blue whales. Blue whales have whalebone plates instead of teeth. The sperm whale, with a large, blunt head, is a fierce fighter. Sperm whales have a mixture of oil and waxy substances in them, which people can use in many ways. As a result, these whales have been hunted for hundreds of years. The humpback whale and the right whale, also hunted for oil and

Humpback whale

Ed Robinson/**TOM STACK & ASSOCIATES**

whalebone, are with the blue whale some of the animals that are in danger of becoming extinct because of overhunting.

The humpback whale is one of the most interesting whales. These mammals live in both the northern and southern hemispheres. Humpback whales *migrate*; that is, they live in different places in summer and winter and follow a regular pattern when they travel. Scientists who have studied this whale say that the animal sings and may use certain repeated phrases to tell stories or to "talk" to other whales. Did you ever use rhyming words to help you remember something? Some scientists say that humpback whales use rhymes in their songs. These songs may last as long as 15 minutes, and some of them have continued for a half hour. What are the whales doing? Do they really send messages in their songs? Do they really use rhymes to help them remember the story? Scientists aren't sure. They do think that these whales are very intelligent mammals.

Dolphin

In the same order as whales are dolphins, which also live in the oceans, and killer whales, which are in the same family as dolphins. Like all mammals, they breathe air through their lungs. Like whales, dolphins must surface often, although they can stay underwater for a long time. Dolphins have shown interest in human beings and seem friendly in most situations. Many dolphins have been taught to perform for audiences and some have been taught to do work for the U.S. Navy. Many scientists consider dolphins to be among the most intelligent animals in the world, next to human beings.

There are other mammals that spend much time in the water, but unlike whales and dolphins, they also live on land. These are the many kinds of seals, sea lions, and walruses that may be found near most coastlines, especially around the Pacific Ocean, on both coasts of South America, and on the southern coast of Australia. These land-and-water animals belong to a different order of mammals.

Opossum

Koalas

A Different Kind of Mammal

One of the earliest kinds of mammals is called a *marsupial*. The marsupial's young are completely helpless when they are born, and the baby is kept in its mother's pouch until it is strong enough to leave. A common marsupial in both South and North America is the opossum, but most marsupials live in Australia where they haven't had to compete with other mammals for food or space.

Australia's marsupials are well-known and show great variety: the kangaroo, with its strong legs and a tail that can be used as a prop, carries its tiny baby, called a joey, in its pouch; a smaller version of the kangaroo is called a wallaby; and perhaps the most famous of Australia's marsupials is the furry koala. The continent is also home to a catlike marsupial called a quoll, and to mice that carry their young in pouches.

Manatee

Other Mammals

There are many other orders of mammals. Some of them live in only one small part of the world. Others are rare. A platypus is a mammal, but there is a difference between it and most mammals: the platypus doesn't give birth to live babies; it lays eggs. However, the mother does feed the hatched babies on milk. The platypus, like many unusual animals, lives in Australia. Two other strange mammals are manatees and dugongs—both of which live in the oceans.

Which of the mammals that you have read about have you seen? Which are native to the place where you live? Which are wild? Domesticated? Which have you seen in a zoo? In a circus? On television or in movies and books? Look at a map. How far would you have to travel to see a whale? A wild lion or a kangaroo? Have you ever seen a woolly mammoth? Why not?

Mastodon

Cave bear

Irish elk

Giant sloth

Woolly rhinoceros

Woolly mammoth

Saber-toothed cat

Mammals of the Past

About 10,000 years ago the last of the glaciers that covered large parts of Earth began to melt. As the ice disappeared, the land changed. As the land changed, the animals that had lived in each kind of place had to find new homes and foods. At that time, hundreds of species of large animals, most of them mammals, became extinct. Among them were mammoths, mastodons, cave bears, saber-toothed cats, ground sloths, Irish elk, woolly rhinoceroses, and giant kangaroos.

Scientists aren't sure why so many of these animals vanished. Maybe it was because of the great changes in weather. Maybe it was because the foods they ate vanished when the land changed. Maybe it was because people moved in when the glaciers melted and they hunted the animals to extinction.

Is extinction part of nature's changes? Do you think it is necessary for some kinds of animals to disappear so there is room for others? What do you think happened to different species of animals when the climate began to change? Some were able to move their homes, traveling away from the changing climate. For example, as a glacier moved into the animal's territory, the animal stayed just ahead of the glacier. You know that any big change in climate, like a glacier moving, would be very, very slow. It would take hundreds of years in most cases.

Other animals would change a little bit to be able to live in the new climate. A few would disappear. But as soon as one kind of animal moves, changes, or disappears, other kinds of animals are also in danger. Maybe the animal that left was part of their food supply. Or maybe that animal was their enemy and hunted them. That kept their numbers down. Once the enemy was gone, their numbers grew and they had no more room or no more food. Every plant and animal in a wild area depends on the other plants and animals that are there. Any change affects all the living things.

Wolves with their prey

Thomas Kitchin/TOM STACK & ASSOCIATES

A deer on the run

If the extinction of some plants and animals has always been part of nature, why are so many people today worried about it?

In recent times extinction of animals has speeded up. In the last 300 years, at least 300 vertebrate animals have become extinct. The cause of this rapid change in the rate of extinction is mostly human activity.

Sometimes people accidentally bring about the extinction of a species. Imagine an island where an unusual animal lives with no enemies. Then people come by ship and decide to live there. They bring pet dogs and it turns out that dogs are enemies of the unusual animal. Soon that animal may be extinct. This kind of thing has happened in real life. Some animals have become extinct by accident when humans moved in. No one meant to destroy them.

A coyote at home

People have caused extinction in two other ways. The first way is by deliberate killing of an animal. Sometimes this has happened because the animal was a pest. Other times it has happened because the humans in the area wanted the animal for meat or clothing or because they just enjoyed hunting it.

Wolves, coyotes, bison, deer, and large cats are some of the mammals killed as pests. Some families of these are extinct. Others are *endangered*. This means that if care isn't taken, they will be extinct. Why would people kill these animals? Sometimes they think the animal is in the way of what they want to do. For instance, a sheep rancher might be afraid that the coyotes, cats, or wolves will kill lambs. A farmer who grows grain wants the bison and deer to stay away from the fields. Sometimes people want to build homes and have yards in an area where wild animals still live. They don't want these animals breaking fences or eating their gardens. So the animals are killed.

In earlier times, animals were often hunted nearly to extinction because they provided good meat, oil, or fur. This happened to the American bison, to whales, and to some reindeer and elk. It is still happening, even though most people today eat meat produced from animals raised on ranches or farms. When a mammal is in danger from hunters today, it is often from people hunting for sport or to sell a valuable product such as fur or ivory. For example, the African elephant is in danger from *poachers*. A poacher is a hunter who goes against the law to kill an animal. The elephant is hunted because people will buy things made from its ivory tusks. Some walruses are hunted for the same reason. Seals are often hunted because people want their fur.

The other way in which people cause the extinction of animals is by destroying their *habitat*. A habitat is the place where an animal lives, finds shelter, water, and food, and raises its young.

Today, wetlands around the world are often drained so people can build homes or farms. Forests are cut down for the same reason. Rivers are moved or dammed to furnish water in deserts so people can live and farm there. These are some examples of how people change habitats and affect animals. What happens to the plants and animals in these places? Some move, some change or adapt, and some become extinct.

Do we care if an animal becomes extinct? Remember that every living thing has some effect on other living things. Does the end of a species of seals faraway affect you? In the end, it probably will. We just don't know how.

Another reason people today worry about the destruction of an animal like the elephant is that they don't want the next generation to grow up without ever seeing one. Imagine Africa without a single elephant or lion anywhere on the continent. Or think of the Antarctic without penguins, the Arctic without polar bears, or Asia without a single panda. Many people don't want this to happen, even if it means that we human beings will have to change some of the things we do to our environment. The care of our environment and its resources, including animals and plants, is called *conservation*.

BIRDS

How is a bird like a buffalo? You know that the buffalo is a mammal, one kind of vertebrate. Birds, too, are vertebrates, and like the buffalo, they are warm-blooded. Both buffalo and birds need a habitat in which they can find food and be safe. Birds are not mammals, however; they belong to a different class of vertebrates.

A bird is a warm-blooded, feathered vertebrate with a beak, two feet (usually with four toes), and two wings. Birds lay eggs from which baby birds will hatch. There are more than 25 orders of birds and they live on every continent and in every ocean on Earth.

Not all birds are alike, though. Like mammals, birds live in different habitats. Each kind of bird has adapted to the way it must live. There are birds that spend their lives in one forest or prairie and there are birds that fly 25,000 miles (40,250 km) every year. There are birds that are nearly always in the air and other birds that can't fly. Some birds live on grain, fruit, and seeds; others eat fish, dead animals, worms, or small animals such as mice and rabbits.

Chicken

Penguin

Over thousands of years, the bodies of some birds have changed. These changes enable each bird to survive in its own way.

What does a chicken eat? How does it get its food? A chicken will scratch in the ground to find grain and small insects. What does a chicken need to live like this? It needs claws that are strong enough to scratch, a beak that can pick up the small seeds, and wings just strong enough to get it into a tree if a fox or other enemy appears. Chickens don't need to fly long distances, so they don't need light bodies and strong wings.

On the other hand, a penguin doesn't need to fly at all. Penguins use their wings like fish use their fins—to move them through the water. Penguins are at home in water, so they need smooth waterproof feathers, beaks that can hold a fish, webbed feet, and coloring that will provide protection from enemies above the water and enemies under the water.

Vultures, which live on *carrion*, or dead animals, need beaks that tear, strong wings to keep them in the air for hours while they search for food, and feet suited to standing on ground rather than perching.

Birds throughout the world have adapted in similar ways to fit their environments.

Migrating storks

Long-distance Fliers

Any animal will move from its native habitat if that habitat can't support it, but some animals travel long distances every year, usually moving from cold weather to warm weather. These animals travel, or migrate, each year between the same two places.

Many birds are migratory and some species travel very long distances. Scientists aren't sure what causes birds to migrate. The birds seem to have a calendar or clock inside that tells them when it is time to begin their long journeys. Perhaps they migrate because their ancestors had to move to find food. Perhaps the changing length of the days tells them it is time to find a warmer climate.

Birds generally move in a north-south pattern, and scientists have identified many flyways, or routes, these birds follow. They often fly high above rivers. In North America, for example, hundreds of thousands of birds, mostly geese and ducks, follow the Mississippi River every spring and every fall. Others may fly along coastlines or mountain chains.

Geese feeding in a cornfield

Willard Luce/Animals

Some birds, such as the arctic tern, fly long distances over water, where there are no landmarks. Scientists believe birds may use sun and star positions and may have a magnetic sense that helps them to know the direction of the north or south pole.

There is another mystery about the migration of birds. It always takes place at the same time. In the northern hemisphere, some species of birds arrive in their northern homes early in March. Others come later, perhaps in April. Birds from farther south will arrive in May. Many of these species will arrive on the same date each year.

As birds migrate, they must find food and they need a great deal of food because they are using so much energy. Birds that eat seeds or insects from the ground are likely to fly by night and spend their days resting and eating. Other birds eat insects that are in the air. They eat as they are flying. These birds will travel whenever they can find food. Water birds may migrate during either the day or night, landing on water or in nearby fields to find food.

Scientists have learned a great deal about migration through banding. Carefully trained volunteers catch birds in a trap or cage. Then they attach a very light band with a number on it around each bird's leg. A record is made of the number, showing the date, place, and kind of bird. This is reported to a central office. The bird is turned loose to continue its journey. Perhaps that bird is caught again. The person who catches it makes a new recording, and the bird's location tells more about where the bird goes and how long the journey takes.

The arctic tern provides an example of how scientists have learned about migration from banding birds. A tern might be banded with a number on May 18 on the coast of Brazil. The same number could be reported on a bird on June 16 in Greenland. Then scientists would know that that bird flew from Brazil to Greenland in about four weeks.

A biologist banding a bird

Jack D. Swenson/**TOM STACK & ASSOCIATES**

An arctic tern in the air

Birds can get more and better food because they migrate, but migration is also dangerous. Storms sometimes cause birds to lose their way. Strong winds blow them against buildings or trees. Late winter storms bring cold weather they can't survive. On long flights, weaker birds can't keep up with the flock. Many birds have to watch out for birds and other animals that are their enemies.

Another danger, especially for ducks and geese, is from hunters who learn the birds' flight patterns and watch for them along the way. Many governments have passed laws prohibiting hunting during the seasons when the birds are passing through.

The arctic tern is the champion of all long-distance fliers. It is a thin bird with webbed feet and pointed wings and tail. The bluish-gray color of its body makes it hard to be seen in the air or over water. The tern is a relative of the sea gulls seen in many parts of the world. Like the gulls, the tern mainly eats fish.

The arctic tern spends almost half of every year traveling. In March the tern leaves its home near Antarctica and flies over 12,000 miles

An arctic tern at its nest

(19,320 km) to the Arctic. Here the warm season is beginning and the short summer will be busy. Each pair of terns builds a simple nest, a hollow place in the sand lined with dry grass or seaweed. The female tern lays three greenish-white eggs spotted with brown, black, and lavender. The tern has just about three months to hatch the eggs and raise its young. By the time the young birds are able to fly, it is August and time to begin the long journey south. The terns arrive back in the southern hemisphere for the warm season near the South Pole. Terns make a round trip of about 25,000 miles (40,250 km) each year.

Many other birds migrate over long distances. The golden plover makes its nest in the northern part of North America and migrates 2,000 miles (3,220 km) south to Argentina every year. Another bird, the shearwater, breeds in the islands near Tasmania south of the mainland of Australia. Then for seven months the birds fly around the Pacific Ocean, feeding as they fly. They go north to Japan and Siberia, across to Alaska, and south along the coast of the United States. Finally, they fly back across the Pacific to their islands.

Migrating birds make their journeys at different speeds. The arctic tern travels about 150 miles (240 km) in a day, while the black-and-white warbler, which flies from Hudson Bay in Canada to Cuba and back, may travel less than 25 miles (40 km) a day.

Among the best-known migrating birds in the northern hemisphere are ducks and geese. Immense flocks of these birds can be heard overhead as they fly north in the spring and head back south in the fall. People who live near wetlands and rivers may see thousands of these birds as they noisily land to feed along the riverbanks or in nearby fields of grain. A famous North American traveler is the sandhill crane, which winters in Texas and nests in the Arctic. Another crane, the whooping crane, also makes this long journey. The whooping crane is an endangered species. Many scientists and bird lovers are watching the survival of this long-legged water bird carefully.

Sandhill crane

Larry Brock/TOM STACK & ASSOCIATES

Robin

Birds Close to Home

The stories of birds that have migrated long distances can make us appreciate these interesting travelers. Most of us, however, are better acquainted with the small birds that live as our neighbors. Some of these are migrants. Others are year-round residents.

The thrush is a medium-sized brown songbird and usually has a spotted breast. It is seen in many countries. In North America, the most common thrush is the robin. Robins can be seen year-round in some parts of the continent, but they are present in the far north only in summer and in the south only in winter. Most robins migrate, however. The birds you see in the winter will head farther north when summer comes. The birds you see in the summer have probably come from farther south.

A robin's nest
and eggs

John Gerlach/TOM STACK & ASSOCIATES

If robins live near you only in summer, watch to see what date they appear on. They will probably come every year at about the same time. Robins often return to nest in the same tree or bush year after year.

The male robin has gray-brown feathers, a black head, and a bright red breast. The female is colored in the same way, but her head and breast are much less bright. This difference in coloring is common among birds. It is the female who will lay eggs and sit on the nest. It is safer for her if she is less brightly colored because she will be less visible to enemies.

Robins build firm nests of mud, twigs, string, and scraps of paper. When the nest is finished, it is shaped like a small bowl. Soon the nest will hold four to six greenish-blue eggs. The mother robin will sit on the eggs for 14 days, leaving only once a day for food and water. When the baby robins hatch, both parents will spend most of their time finding worms to bring to the young.

Baby robins grow fast. In about 11 days they are almost covered with feathers. But their breasts are spotted, like those of most thrushes, not red like their parents' breasts.

When their wing feathers are big enough, the young birds will leave their nests. At first they flutter among the low branches or on the ground. After a few attempts, they can use their wings better but may have trouble keeping their balance because their tail feathers are still short and stubby. By fall, the young robins have grown full-sized wing and tail feathers. They are ready to make the trip south.

Grasshoppers, beetles, earthworms, and cutworms are an important part of a robin's diet. You will see the birds gather near a sprinkler because water soaking into the ground forces worms to come to the surface where the robin can get at them. Robins also eat fruit. Wild fruits such as mulberries and raspberries attract them. They also eat cherries. As a result, people who grow cherries consider the robins pests. However, since robins eat harmful cutworms and grasshoppers, they really do more good than harm in their environment.

Another familiar bird is the woodpecker. Every continent except Antarctica is home to some member of the woodpecker family. In many ways all of its members are alike. They all have sharp, strong bills and short, stubby tails. Their legs are short, and most woodpeckers have four toes on each foot, two of them pointing forward and two pointing backward. Most woodpeckers are black and white, trimmed with red. There are some differences, of course. For example, the arctic woodpecker has three toes on each foot and yellow trim instead of red. The flicker, another common woodpecker, also has some yellow and is more brown than black.

Watch a woodpecker on a tree and you will see why the woodpecker has toes pointing both forward and backward and why its tail is short and stubby. The bird's sharp claws dig into the bark of a tree; the back-pointing toes and the strong tail help it to balance.

Redheaded woodpecker

Marcia W. Griffen/Animals Animals

Why are woodpeckers usually seen on the sides of trees or poles? Most woodpeckers eat insects, insect eggs, and caterpillars. They hold onto the sides of trees and peck at the wood in front of them. With bills like chisels, they take out little chips of wood as they cut their way into the tree. Soon the woodpecker reaches an insect which it brings out with its long tongue. A woodpecker's tongue is three or four times as long as its beak and is barbed at the end.

When the bird stops tapping, it may be listening for insects in the tree trunk, a sound no person could hear. When it pecks at the tree, it has located something to eat. Because woodpeckers eat so many insects that are harmful to trees, they are usually helpful members of the forest community.

However, one type of woodpecker, the sapsucker, sometimes drills so many holes in one tree that the tree dies. The sapsucker isn't searching for insects but for sap and, since its tongue isn't long, it often drills deeply into the trunk to get to the sap.

Sometimes, after woodpeckers have pecked and chipped their way into the insects' homes, they keep on pecking and chipping until the holes have become big enough for the birds to fit inside. There they will work until the space is about a foot (30 cm) deep and is lined with very fine wood chips on the bottom. This is the way most woodpeckers make their nests.

Four or five white eggs are laid on the soft bed of chips in the nest. When the babies hatch, they look like most bird babies—pink and featherless with huge beaks and mouths. The parent birds feed them insects and larvae.

Many woodpeckers are permanent residents in the areas where they live. The holes in trees make warm, safe nests even in winter. Some woodpeckers migrate, however. Of the two most common North American woodpeckers, one, the downy woodpecker, is a permanent resident and the other, the redheaded woodpecker, is a migrant.

Like many animals, woodpeckers have family members that specialize, or live in only one type of habitat. The pileated woodpecker, a very large bird, lives in evergreen forests. The ivory-billed woodpecker, almost two feet (0.6 m) long, is thought by some scientists to be extinct. Others list it as endangered. Its habitat, the thick cypress forest in Cuba and the United States, has been cleared except for a few small areas. This beautiful bird is the victim of human activity.

The downy woodpecker, which is only about six inches (15 cm) long, is not specialized. Downys will live in almost any type of tree.

Woodpeckers are easy to identify because a bird watcher can hear the *peck, peck, peck* if one is in the area.

Downy woodpecker

John Gerlach/**TOM STACK & ASSOCIATES**

Pileated woodpecker

Marcia W. Griffen/Animals Animals

Ostriches

Birds That Cannot Fly

Millions of years ago, most scientists believe, all of the continents were joined. During that time a type of bird developed in the southern part of that huge continent. It was a flightless bird—the kind called a *ratite* today. When the continents began to separate, some of the ratites were on each of the southern continents—Africa, Australia, and South America—and on New Zealand. Today five species of ratites live in those places.

The ostrich is the largest bird in the world. It is Africa's ratite. A full-grown ostrich may weigh as much as 300 pounds (135 kg). The ostrich's huge body makes it difficult for the bird to raise itself from the ground and fly. On long strong legs, the ostrich can outrun most of its enemies, reaching about 45 miles (72 km) an hour. Over the centuries, the bird began to depend on its legs more and its wings less. So the wings grew smaller as the rest of the bird increased in size. Ostriches do use their wings, however, to help them in turning and stopping.

Ostrich nests are simple; the birds scoop out a shallow place in warm sand. An ostrich usually lays about 15 eggs, but the eggs of many females are often laid in the same nest so there may be as many as 50 eggs in one place. The sand and sun usually keep the eggs warm enough during the day, and one ostrich will watch over them. The feathers on the underside of a female ostrich are white, but above, where the feathers are visible to enemies, she is dull gray—almost the color of the sand around her. At night, the male ostrich sits on the nest. His back is black and can't be easily seen in the dark.

Ostrich eggs are sometimes used as food by people, who take them from the nests. An ostrich egg weighs about three pounds (1.35 kg). In about six or seven weeks, the baby ostriches hatch. They are about the size of a grown chicken and can follow their parents about in just a few hours. The babies grow fast and in six months are almost as large as their parents, but they aren't completely grown until they are about three years old. Young ostriches are dull yellow, and they don't have the long beautiful plumes of the adults.

Ostriches eat mostly plant parts, such as leaves, stems, seeds, and fruits. They protect themselves by kicking. A kick from the strong legs of an ostrich is about as powerful as one from a horse. An ostrich may live to be 80 years old.

Animals Animals

Cassowary

Ostriches, like most birds, can make noise, but no one would consider an ostrich noise a song! It sounds more like a lion's roar. Ostriches also have a movement that is almost like a dance. They fluff up their feathers, hold open their wings, and whirl around in circles. Many birds may dance at the same time.

For a long time, ostriches were in danger of extinction because their beautiful plumes were in demand for hats and decorations. Today the wild birds are protected by law, and many ostriches are raised on farms. Once or twice a year the plumes are clipped from these tame birds and new ones grow. Although ostriches may be raised on farms, they can't be completely tamed and remain suspicious of people.

South America's ratite bird is the rhea. It is smaller than an ostrich and lives in the southern half of the continent. The emu, which lives in Australia, is also smaller than the ostrich and doesn't have the long white plumes. The cassowary of Australia is brown with blue and red around its head. The kiwi, which lives on the islands of New Zealand, is a small ratite, little larger than a chicken. It has no tail, very tiny wings, and nostrils at the end of its long skinny beak.

Hummingbirds

Many families of birds, like the thrushes, woodpeckers, and the ostrich and its relatives, are found on many continents. The tiny hummingbird, however, is found only in North and South America.

The hummingbird is the smallest of all American birds and can move in ways no other bird can. A hummingbird can fly straight up, forward, and backward, and when flying forward, may reach a speed of a mile (1.6 km) a minute. The hummingbird can also *hover*, or fly in place, but it can't walk or run. Its feet are so tiny, it can perch only on very small twigs.

There are many species of hummingbirds. One, the ruby-throated hummingbird, is seen frequently in parts of the United States. Its heart can beat as fast as 60 times a second as it hovers over a flower. The wings of the bird move so fast, they can hardly be seen. It is the sound made by the hummingbird's vibrating wings that gives it its name.

Hummingbirds live on the nectar from flowers. They also suck small insects in the nectar. The hummingbird has a long sharp beak and a long tongue. The sides of the bird's tongue roll in toward the center, making it into two tubes. The bird runs this two-tube tongue down into

the sweet nectar of a flower, drinking it much like we would use a straw. Honeysuckles, trumpet vines, phlox, and gladiolas are among the flowers that have the nectar the hummingbird needs. People who are interested in hummingbirds sometimes put out hummingbird feeders. A bright red feeder holding sweetened water will attract the birds.

Hummingbirds can also use their sharp beaks as weapons. They often fight among themselves, and in spite of their small size, the birds will also attack other birds many times larger. A crow or hawk will avoid a fight with a hummingbird. It knows it has little chance against the fast, sharp-beaked little bird that can attack from any angle.

A hummingbird's cup-shaped nest is about the size of a thimble. It is made of plant parts and lined with milkweed or dandelion down. The bird fastens the nest to a branch with threads of spider webs, moss, or lichen. The female bird lays two tiny white eggs and cares for the babies that hatch.

Hummingbirds are migrants. They may travel from the northern part of North America to Central America, crossing the Gulf of Mexico without stopping.

Dodo, an extinct bird

Birds in Danger

You know that many mammals have become extinct in modern times. Most of these have disappeared because of the activities of human beings. The same thing is true of birds. The dodo is probably the best-known example of a bird that is gone forever. Dodos lived on the island of Mauritius. About 500 years ago, sailors began stopping there on the long voyages between Europe and the East Indies. They found the large flightless birds were very good to eat. Besides, the birds were easy to kill because they had never had enemies and weren't afraid. Ships began to stop at the island on every trip in order to get fresh meat. Within 200 years there was not a single dodo left on Earth. Because every living thing depends on others, a kind of tree also became extinct on Mauritius. It had needed the dodo to spread its seeds.

Many other birds have disappeared forever. Among them are some species of ducks, herons, cranes, doves, parrots, and wrens. Other species are endangered. Nearly all of these birds were affected by human activity. What do people do that causes extinction? Here are some endangered birds and the reasons they are in trouble.

The Amsterdam albatross, which lives in the area of the Indian Ocean, has lost its habitat because of fires and overgrazing by cattle. Also, people have introduced dogs and cats, enemies of the albatross.

A beautiful Oriental white stork, whose habitat is in China, Japan, the USSR, and South Korea, is in danger because of pesticides and the draining of the wet places it needs for its habitat.

In the United States, the California condor has almost disappeared from the wild. The reason is not certain; perhaps the big birds have been crowded out by people moving into their habitat or interfering with their source of food. Another possible cause is the way pesticides affect the food they eat.

There are long lists of extinct and endangered birds. All over the world, scientists and other concerned people are studying the causes of the problems and are trying to think of solutions.

California condor

M. A. Chappell/Animals Animals

Reptiles, like mammals and birds, have backbones, but they aren't warm-blooded and they aren't covered with feathers or fur. Reptiles are cold-blooded, scaly vertebrates with short legs or with no legs at all. Reptiles usually reproduce by laying eggs.

There are three large orders of reptiles: crocodiles and alligators, snakes and lizards, and turtles and tortoises. Animals from each of these orders may be found in most parts of the world.

Scales are small overlapping pieces of hardened membrane that cover the body of a reptile. The scales of some reptiles are soft and flexible while others are thick and hard and form a shell.

Reptiles are cold-blooded. This means their body temperatures change with the temperature of their surroundings. Because they are cold-blooded, they require less food than do animals that keep their body temperatures at the same level all the time.

Snake

Lizard

Snakes and Lizards

Snakes and lizards are members of one order in the class of reptiles. The body of a snake is covered with dry scales. On the underside of the body, the scales are fastened by muscles to the tips of the ribs. Snakes use these muscles to raise the free edges of their scales. As the muscles pull on the scales, the edges of the scales push against the ground, moving the snake forward. A snake may have more than 200 pairs of these ribs with the muscles attached.

Because the snake's scales push against the ground, it can move much faster on rough ground than on a smooth surface. A snake would have great difficulty moving on a hard, slick rock.

Snakes can also move by throwing their bodies into wavelike curves. Some snakes move so fast they are called racers. Others climb trees. Some snakes swim well and spend much of their lives in water. Snakes and a few lizards are the only reptiles that have no legs.

The food source for most snakes is smaller animals, such as mice, gophers, toads, frogs, and insects. Some large snakes may eat deer or pigs. Snakes swallow their food whole. Some kill their prey first. Others swallow it alive.

Snakes may kill their prey in one of two ways. Some, such as the huge boa constrictors and anacondas of South America and the pythons of southeastern Asia, wrap the coils of their bodies around animals, suffocating them. Anacondas and pythons are sometimes more than 30 feet (9 m) long. A snake of this size can easily kill a full-grown deer or a large wild pig. Other snakes kill animals by stabbing them with needlelike hollow teeth to inject poison. After a snake has eaten, it may wait as long as a week before it needs to eat again.

A boa constrictor eating a mouse

John Cancalosi/TOM STACK & ASSOCIATES

Fangs and venom of a rattlesnake

Snakes are able to swallow animals larger than they are because their upper and lower jaws are held together by elastic ligaments, or bands, which stretch to allow the jaws to open wide. The bones of the lower jaws, and in some snakes the bones of both jaws, are fastened at the tip of the mouth by the same kind of bands. These bands stretch to make the snake's mouth much larger when it swallows something. If the snake is swallowing a live animal, it holds the prey with its fine, sharp teeth. These teeth are curved so that food can't slip out of the snake's mouth.

Poisonous snakes have some of their upper teeth connected with poison glands. These teeth are grooved or hollow to carry the venom from the glands. In some snakes, there may be only one very large hollow tooth on each side. These teeth are called poison fangs. Some of these fangs are more than half an inch (1.25 cm) long.

Rattlesnake

W. Perry Conway/TOM STACK & ASSOCIATES

Copperhead

Joe & Carol McDonald/TOM STACK & ASSOCIATES

Most snakes aren't poisonous. Four kinds of poisonous snakes live in the United States: rattlesnakes, water moccasins, copperheads, and coral snakes. Rattlesnakes are found in most parts of the country. The rattle, a series of hard, dry rings of skin, vibrates when the snake coils to strike. The water moccasin lives mostly in swampy areas in the southern United States. The copperhead, another poisonous snake, is closely related to the moccasin.

The coral snake is common in the southeastern part of the United States. It has a bright coral color trimmed with black. It is a beautiful but deadly reptile. The coral snake has a relative that lives in India, the poisonous cobra.

Snakes may lose or shed teeth, but new ones quickly grow in to take their place. Snakes have long forked tongues with slender tips. The tongue moves rapidly in and out of the snake's mouth. Snakes use their tongues to feel and touch things, much as people use their fingers.

When snakes grow, their skins don't grow with them. Rather, the snake will shed its skin and grow a new one. Some snakes need new skins several times a year. Even the eyes of a snake are covered with a thin, transparent skin which is also shed.

Snakes don't have eyelids and so they can't close their eyes. Because snakes don't walk like other animals, because their tongues flick in and out constantly, and because they can't blink but seem to stare, many people fear and dislike them. Snakes, however, are important animals in any part of the world. There are very few snakes that are dangerous to humans, and snakes control the small animals that might otherwise become pests.

Most female snakes lay eggs. They may crawl into a crevice or between stones or bushes to deposit the eggs. The snake will leave the eggs to be warmed by the sun. A baby snake opens its shell with a sharp point on the tip of its snout. This point is called an egg tooth. Soon after the snake hatches, the point disappears. Baby snakes are able to care for themselves as soon as they are hatched.

Rattlesnakes differ from most snakes. They don't lay eggs. The baby snakes are born alive—12 or more at a time. These babies are also ready to care for themselves immediately. Garter snakes also bear live young.

Even though most snakes are harmless, they have ways of protecting themselves. For instance, many have protective coloring. A green grass snake is almost the color of the grass where it lives. Brown spotted snakes look like the ground under them. Some snakes are able to crawl so fast they can escape most enemies, and others slide into protected places at any sign of danger.

In colder climates, snakes find holes or cracks when autumn comes. There they sleep for the winter. This winter sleep is called *hibernation*. Large numbers of snakes may gather in such places. When spring comes, they come out of their sleeping places and begin to hunt for food.

Snapping turtle

Reptiles with Shells

What do you already know about turtles? You can be sure of these facts: turtles are reptiles; they have shells, heads, and four feet. Turtles, however, are different from each other in many ways. Some are very small. Others may be eight feet (2.4 m) long. Some turtles are the color of mud; others look as though they have been covered with red or yellow paint.

Some turtles live in water nearly all of their lives, while others live on land. Most turtles, however, live partly on land and partly in the water. A turtle that lives on land is a *tortoise*. Those that live in ponds, rivers, and swamps are called *terrapins*, or mud turtles. Terrapins are often used for food. All of these animals are turtles.

A turtle's shell may be dome-shaped or flat. The shell is usually made of a bony box covered with horny scales, but some turtles have only leathery skin over the bone. Turtles that live in water have webbed feet.

There are many kinds of turtles and they are found all over the world. The box turtle lives on land, usually near dry woods. The pond turtle is very small and is sometimes kept in garden pools as a pet. The giant tortoise of the Galápagos Islands in the Pacific Ocean may weigh 400 pounds (180 kg) and live for more than 100 years.

One of the most common and best-known turtles is the snapping turtle. It gets its name from the way it snaps its jaws together. Its head seems to move as fast as lightning and its jaws can remove a careless person's finger. There are no teeth in these powerful jaws; no turtles have teeth. Instead the jaws have horny ridges which are very sharp.

A snapping turtle has a large head and a long tail that looks somewhat like an alligator's tail. Its legs have flabby folds of dirt-colored skin around them and its feet are webbed. The snapping turtle's rough shell is a dull brown, which makes good camouflage since the turtle spends much of its time in the mud. Sometimes moss grows on the turtle's back and helps make it look like a big rock at the edge of the water. This turtle's shell may grow to be more than a foot (30 cm) long.

Rivers and lakes are the usual homes for snapping turtles. They swim well. Like all turtles, they must breathe above water. Snapping turtles eat smaller water animals and birds. They catch and eat their prey in the water. They seem to swallow only when their heads are underwater.

Once a year, in spring, a female snapper will leave her home at the water's edge to go on land. Here she will find a soft place in the earth and dig with her back legs until her body is partially buried in the dirt. There she lays about 25 hard-shelled, round white eggs. They are about half the size of chicken eggs. She remains there, laying eggs, for several days. After the eggs are laid, the turtle will scratch dirt over them and return to the water.

The turtle eggs stay in the hole in the ground for several weeks. When the eggs are ready to hatch, the baby turtles break through the egg with their egg teeth. They push, turn, and twist their way out, sometimes taking several hours. As soon as the baby turtles are hatched, they make their way to the water. There they are ready to care for and feed themselves.

Snapping turtles hibernate deep in the mud at the bottom of a pond. They lie there until spring comes.

There is one unusually large kind of snapping turtle called the alligator snapping turtle. It is the largest land or freshwater turtle in North America. It is found in the Mississippi River and in many rivers in the southern part of the United States.

Many turtles live in the oceans of the world. The green turtle lives in warm ocean areas. One population of green turtles lives in the warm, shallow waters off the coast of Brazil. Here the turtles feed on eelgrass and algae. Every year these turtles make an amazing journey as they migrate 1,240 miles (1,996 km) across the Atlantic to a small island called Ascension Island. Here, in December, the turtles lay their eggs in the sand. The babies take 10 weeks to emerge. All of them hatch at the same time, at night, and scramble to the sea. No one completely understands why the turtles make their long migration every year.

Young green turtles

George H.H. Huey/Animals Animals

Crocodile

Alligator

Giant Reptiles

The crocodile and the alligator in the pictures are the largest living reptiles. Alligators may grow to be about 15 feet (4.5 m) long and crocodiles grow even longer. Like all reptiles, alligators and crocodiles come from eggs. Except for some sharks, the crocodile is the largest living creature that hatches from an egg.

Both the crocodile and the alligator have leathery skin and their backs are covered with hard bony scales. They have huge mouths and powerful jaws with rows of sharp teeth. These teeth, like those of other reptiles, can be replaced. Each tooth is shaped like a cone, with the point of a new tooth growing up inside the old one. When the old tooth comes out, a new one is there to take its place.

Alligators and crocodiles have strange tongues. The tongues of most animals are fastened at the back of the mouth. A toad's tongue is fastened at the front. But these reptiles' tongues are fastened on the underside all the way around. The tongues can be raised and lowered to squeeze water out of the reptiles' mouths.

When a crocodile or alligator is underwater, it can raise a fleshy valve at the back of its mouth and close its throat. In this way, the reptile can open its huge mouth when it needs to without swallowing water. These reptiles can also protect their ears from water by closing a bony flap that grows over each ear.

Both reptiles are strong swimmers, but they don't use their feet when swimming as most animals do. They hold their feet close to their bodies, making themselves more streamlined. Then they push through the water by flipping their big tails from side to side. These long, strong tails are also powerful weapons and can strike terrific blows that will stun even large animals such as cattle or deer.

The female crocodile or alligator leaves the water and crawls onto land when it is time to lay eggs. She may dig a hole in the sand or she may build a mound of twigs, leaves, and moss. The eggs are white and have hard shells. About two or three dozen eggs are laid, usually in several layers. Between the layers, the reptile will place mud, leaves, and grass and cover the entire nest when she is through. As soon as the eggs are laid, the reptile returns to the water.

The sun and the rotting leaves and grass keep the eggs warm. The baby alligators, when they hatch, are black with yellow markings. Crocodile babies are greenish-brown with black markings. As the babies grow up, they lose the markings.

These baby reptiles eat fish and other animals that live in water. The adults eat fish, too, but they also catch land animals that come to the water's edge to drink.

Crocodiles and alligators are much alike, but they differ in a few ways. You can recognize each animal because the crocodile has a narrow head and a pointed snout, and its teeth show even when its mouth is closed. The alligator's head is broad, its snout is rounded, and when its mouth is closed, its teeth don't show.

Alligators and crocodiles prefer warm climates, but the alligator can stand more cold than can a crocodile, so it is often found a little farther north. Alligators live only in the southeastern part of the United States and in China. These reptiles spend the winters buried in mud in the rivers and swamps where they live.

Crocodiles live in the warm rivers of South America, Africa, and Asia. The only crocodile in North America lives in the swamps of the southern tip of Florida.

Crocodiles hatching

D. G. Barker/TOM STACK & ASSOCIATES

Reptiles in Danger

The most famous of all extinct animals are the dinosaurs, many of which are related to modern-day reptiles. These amazing animals died out gradually, over a period of millions of years. In more recent times some smaller reptiles have become extinct, and many reptiles all over the world are now endangered animals.

One reason crocodiles, alligators, and some snakes are in danger is because of their thick patterned skins. Hunters have killed these animals in order to sell the skins for shoes, purses, belts, billfolds, and other articles. Uncontrolled hunting brought some of the reptiles close to extinction. The other main danger to the reptiles is the loss of their habitat when people change the wet areas these animals must have in order to live.

Alligators

Brian Parker/TOM STACK & ASSOCIATES

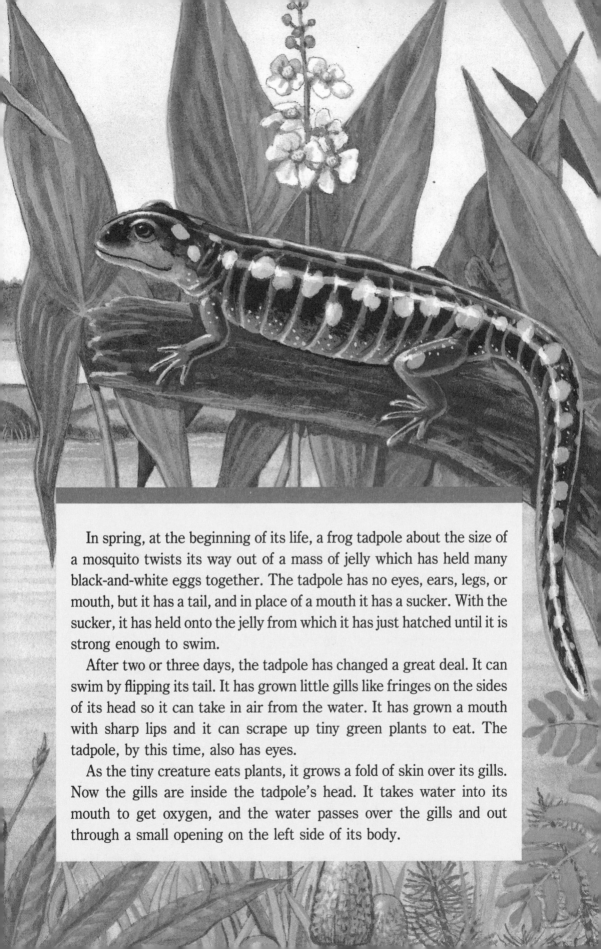

In spring, at the beginning of its life, a frog tadpole about the size of a mosquito twists its way out of a mass of jelly which has held many black-and-white eggs together. The tadpole has no eyes, ears, legs, or mouth, but it has a tail, and in place of a mouth it has a sucker. With the sucker, it has held onto the jelly from which it has just hatched until it is strong enough to swim.

After two or three days, the tadpole has changed a great deal. It can swim by flipping its tail. It has grown little gills like fringes on the sides of its head so it can take in air from the water. It has grown a mouth with sharp lips and it can scrape up tiny green plants to eat. The tadpole, by this time, also has eyes.

As the tiny creature eats plants, it grows a fold of skin over its gills. Now the gills are inside the tadpole's head. It takes water into its mouth to get oxygen, and the water passes over the gills and out through a small opening on the left side of its body.

During the next weeks, the tadpole continues to grow and change. In place of gills, lungs grow. Without gills, the small animal can't breathe underwater so it swims to the surface and begins to breathe air.

Near the tadpole's tail, two small legs appear. In a few more days the hind legs have grown large and front feet begin to develop. By this time, the tadpole can climb among the plants in the pond and can live on land for a few minutes at a time.

While its legs are getting longer, its tail is getting shorter because while tadpoles are growing, they live on food stored in their tails. The tadpole's eyes are beginning to bulge. Its mouth is growing big and it has a tongue. Soon the tadpole will sit on the edge of the pond and will be able to catch and eat grasshoppers and worms. The tadpole will have become a frog.

A frog's tongue is fastened at the front of its mouth and points down its throat. When an insect flies near the frog's mouth, the long sticky tongue flips out, full length. The insect is almost sure to stick to the tip of the tongue.

The little frog will eat a great deal and grow so big that it will have to shed its skin several times as it becomes adult in size. All summer it will eat insects and worms. Then when winter comes, the frog will find a soft, muddy place at the edge of the pond. There it will wiggle its way down into the mud and go to sleep. While it sleeps, the frog will breathe through its skin and use the stored-up food in its body. The frog is hibernating.

When another spring comes, the frog will come up out of the mud. First it will find a mate; then the frogs will find a hidden place in the shallow water where the female will lay several thousand eggs. The frogs will then begin to search for food. The eggs that have been laid will become another generation of tadpoles.

Animals that begin their lives in water, breathing through gills, and then develop lungs and live on land, are called *amphibians*. Frogs and toads are amphibians.

A frog catching a grasshopper

Toad

Toads are like frogs in many ways. Both of them are cold-blooded and spend part of their lives in water and part on land. Neither adult has a tail and their bodies are short and stubby. The front legs are short and are used for balance. The long, stout back legs are useful for jumping and swimming and for digging. Frogs and toads sometimes dig themselves down into the ground, moving backward.

Frogs and toads can see in almost every direction. Their eyes, which look like dark, shiny beads, seem to pop from their heads. When their eyes close, one pair of eyelids moves up from the bottom and another pair moves down from the top. The top eyelids are so small and tight, they push the eyes of the toads and frogs down into their heads. Then their eyes can't be injured easily.

Toads and frogs swallow their food whole. Sometimes they catch such big worms they must use their front feet to cram the worms into their mouths. Frogs have a row of tiny teeth in the upper jaw, but toads have no teeth at all.

All tadpoles are hatched from tiny black-and-white eggs laid in ponds. Toads' eggs are held together in strings of jelly. Frogs' eggs are held in a mass or ball of jelly. The jelly protects the eggs.

Toad tadpoles are black and change into toads when they are very small, while frog tadpoles may be one of several colors and grow to a much larger size before legs appear. Adult frogs and toads are also different. The toad's skin is rough while the frog's skin is smooth, moist, and shiny.

There are many kinds of frogs and toads. Leopard frogs are small and grayish-green with black spots. They blend in with the grass in which they live. They also protect themselves by their ability to jump a distance about 15 times greater than their length. The leopard frog can puff itself up until it is plump and it moistens its skin until it becomes slick. A jumping frog that is slick and plump isn't easy to catch or hold, so its enemies don't find it an easy meal.

Bullfrogs are about twice the size of the leopard frog, about eight inches (20 cm) long. They are greenish-brown and have yellow throats. The bullfrog babies are tadpoles for more than two years before becoming frogs. They hibernate in winter, just as adult bullfrogs do. Bullfrogs, known for their noisy summer evening concerts, croak by forcing air back and forth past their vocal chords. This is how all frogs make sounds.

There are several kinds of small frogs called tree frogs. Some of them change color to blend with the color of the plant they are resting on. This is a great protection because it makes them almost invisible to their enemies. Tree frogs climb trees and walk on smooth surfaces because their toes have pads that help them stick to surfaces. Tree frogs do most of their moving about in the evening. They jump from branch to branch, catching insects with their long sticky tongues. They also do most of their croaking or singing in the evening or when the air grows humid before a rain. Tree frogs, although very small, can make a surprisingly loud noise.

There are amphibians other than frogs and toads. Salamanders are the most common of these. Adult salamanders look like smooth lizards, with thin bodies and long tails which can be replaced if they are pulled off. Most salamanders are small, but a giant salamander in Japan may grow to be five feet (1.5 m) long.

FISH

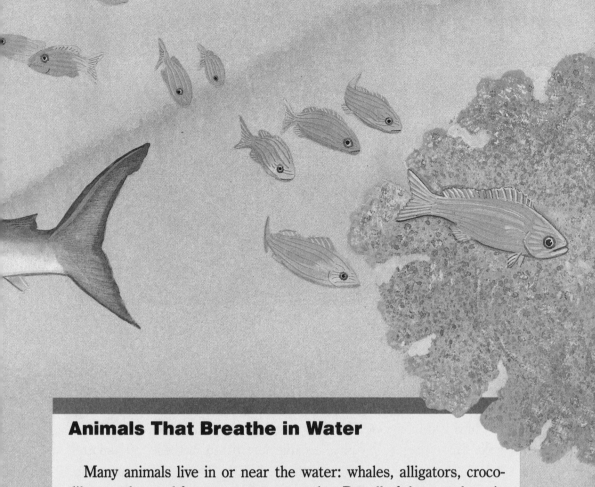

Animals That Breathe in Water

Many animals live in or near the water: whales, alligators, croco-diles, turtles, and frogs are some examples. But all of these, at least in their adult stages, must obtain oxygen from air. Fish are different. They obtain their oxygen from the water by drawing the water through their gills.

There are more fish in the world than any other kind of animal. Almost everywhere there is water, some kind of fish can be found. Some fish live only in cold water, others in warm. Some can live only in lakes and rivers; others are found in just one part of the ocean. Fish eat a variety of foods, everything from microscopic plants to other fish. Fish may be as tiny as a half inch (1.25 cm) or as long as 60 feet (18 m). Fish are so different from one another that it is sometimes difficult to identify them. Most fish belong to one of two groups—fish with bones and fish with cartilage. *Cartilage* is a tough, flexible tissue softer than bone. Sharks belong to the group of fish with cartilage. Fish such as trout, perch, cod, catfish, and salmon are bony fish.

Zig Leszczynski/Animals Animals

From Green to Gold

Hundreds of years ago, small green bony fish swam wild in the rivers of China and Japan. Occasionally, one of these fish would show spots of gold. Some people in China became interested in these gold-spotted fish. They caught one with a little gold color. Then they searched for another to be its mate. When the eggs hatched, many of the young fish also had gold spots. Those that had the most gold were again mated with gold-spotted fish. As each generation of fish grew, more and more gold was visible. Eventually, all of the fish raised were completely gold. Today we have millions of aquariums in all parts of the world with beautiful golden fish swimming in them.

By carefully selecting fish with certain qualities, other fish were bred. Fish descended from the goldfish raised in this way are all called goldfish, but some are black, silver, or spotted, not gold. Goldfish with odd eyes or fancy tails have also been developed. Now decorative goldfish are raised in many parts of the world.

If you have watched goldfish, you know they seem to be swallowing water as they swim. As the gill covers on the sides of the fish's head open and close, water is taken into the fish's mouth, but it isn't swallowed. When it passes back over the gill covers, the gills take oxygen from the water.

Goldfish are adapted to a water habitat in other ways. The body of the fish is streamlined to cut through water easily. Scales on its body overlap like the shingles on a roof. Placed with their edges toward the back, they don't catch the water as the fish moves ahead. Thus the scales protect its body without hindering the fish in any of its movements.

These fish, of course, don't have arms or legs. Instead, they have other parts that help them move in the water. The fish's tail acts like a paddle or propeller. As the tail flips back and forth pushing against the water, it makes the fish move forward.

Goldfish have fins. The back fin and the single fin on the underside of the body are the steering fins. They guide the fish through the water. The fish's side fins, called paired fins, help it to keep its balance and can be used as brakes.

Most fish have eyes but no eyelids. Their eyes are kept clean and moist by the water. Fish have ears, but these are inside their bodies. They can hear sounds that are carried through water, but their sense of hearing isn't as good as that of many other animals. Fish have a sense of smell.

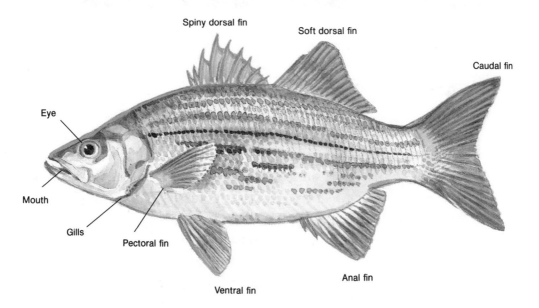

Spiny dorsal fin
Soft dorsal fin
Caudal fin
Eye
Mouth
Gills
Pectoral fin
Ventral fin
Anal fin

A Fish That Migrates

Early in spring, under the surface of the Pacific Ocean, another bony fish, a big salmon about five feet (1.5 m) long, was beginning its long trip up the Columbia River on the western coast of the United States. The salmon, called chinook, or king, salmon, was just one of many fish preparing to make the trip. Most of them weighed about 25 pounds (11.3 kg). A few, however, like the five-foot salmon, might weigh up to 100 pounds (45 kg).

Chinook salmon live and grow for several years in the Pacific Ocean. When they are fully grown, they are ready to leave the salt water of the ocean. For a while they rest and eat as much as they can. Once they begin their migration, they will do no more eating.

Somehow these fish know when it is time to go. Great numbers of them, shiny and silver-colored, swim to the mouth of the Columbia River. They begin to swim upriver—against the current of the river. Huge masses of them splash and leap, rushing and bumping into one another. This migration of salmon is called a salmon run.

In a few days, as they get farther upstream and away from the salt water, the salmon lose their silver color and turn brown. On and on they swim, without stopping for food. They live on the fat they stored up while they were in the Pacific.

Sometimes the swimming isn't hard. At other times, the masses of fish swim into swift currents that seem to push them backward faster than they can go ahead. Occasionally they swim into swift whirlpools that spin them around. But each day they manage to get a little farther upriver.

Some of the salmon can't complete the trip but swim until they die. Others turn up small branches, or tributaries, of the river. Many continue up the main river—a distance of a thousand miles (1,610 k) or more.

On the way upstream, chinook salmon face waterfalls and rapids. The fish must leap high, sometimes six feet (2 m) or more, to get over the falls. It often takes more than one leap to succeed and the salmon are bruised and cut as they fall on rocks. The salmon will jump over and over until they succeed.

Human interference with rivers and streams has had an effect on the salmon run. At Bonneville, almost a hundred miles (161 km) from the Pacific, the fish come to a huge concrete dam across the Columbia River. The engineers who built the dam also built fish ladders and locks to help the salmon continue their journey.

A fish ladder at Bonneville Dam, Columbia River, Oregon

Breck P. Kent/Earth Scenes

Why do salmon make this exhausting journey? The salmon are swimming to breeding grounds that have been used by the chinooks for centuries. As soon as they arrive, female fish begin to look for a place to lay their eggs. In the river, where there is a gravel bottom, the fish uses her head and tail to hollow out a nest. Here she lays several hundred pink eggs about the size of peas. The male fish swims behind her, leaving a milky liquid called milt on the eggs. This fertilizes them so they can hatch. Each female fish makes nest after nest until her several thousand eggs have been laid and fertilized. Each nest is dug a little farther up the river so that the gravel thrown up in digging the nest drifts gently back to cover the newly laid eggs and make them safe. This process of laying and fertilizing eggs is called *spawning*.

Fish don't look after their eggs or the baby fish that hatch. As soon as the eggs are spawned, the big fish turn and begin their return trip down the Columbia River toward the Pacific. The fish haven't eaten since leaving the ocean and they are exhausted. They let the current carry them, tail first, downstream. Within a few hours, most are dead and none live to reach the ocean again.

Many of the salmon eggs are eaten by other animals. Many of the little fish that hatch are also eaten. But some baby salmon survive. As soon as it has hatched, each young fish begins to swim. It lives on the yolk of the egg from which it hatched and which hangs on the underside of its body. When the yolk is gone, the fish begins to feed itself, and when it is two or three inches (5-8 cm) long, it starts downstream. The fast current carries the hundreds of young fish over the falls and out to the Pacific where their parents started. In a few years, these same fish will swim back upstream to spawn and die. How will they know where to go? The migration of these salmon is another migration mystery.

ANIMALS WITHOUT BACKBONES

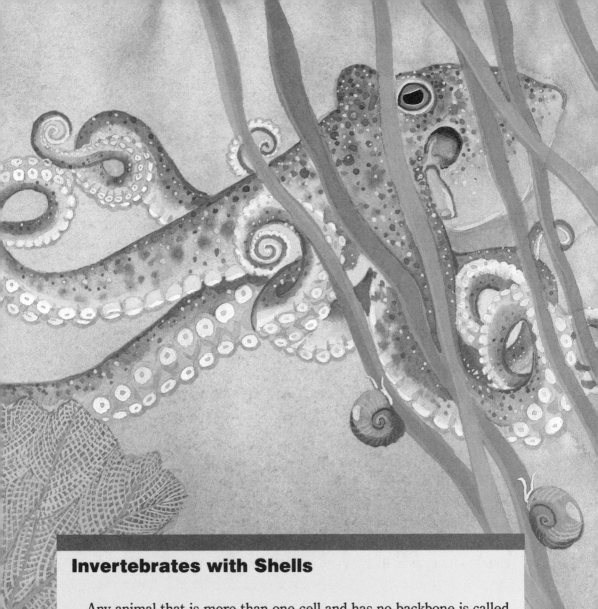

Invertebrates with Shells

Any animal that is more than one cell and has no backbone is called an *invertebrate*. This group is made up of all animals that are not mammals, amphibians, fish, birds, or reptiles. Like the vertebrates, invertebrates can also be divided into many groups.

Many groups of invertebrates live in the water. Animals in one of these groups live between two hard shells. They are called *bivalves*. They have soft bodies and a powerful foot that helps them to move around or to cling. Clams, scallops, mussels, and oysters are well-known bivalves.

The oyster is an animal which has a mouth, lips, heart, and gills but no head, hands, or feet. It looks like a lump of soft flesh between a hinged pair of shells. The shells open and close like the covers of a book. The shells are controlled by strong muscles within the soft body of the animal and by a tough ribbonlike band which hinges the two parts of the shell. This band pulls the shell open. The muscles pull the shell closed.

Oysters can get along without feet because they spend most of their lives fastened to something solid at the bottom of the ocean. They can't move about to search for food, but the ocean water supplies them with both food and oxygen. Oysters live along the ocean shores in bays or at the mouths of rivers. The depth of the water in which they live may be very shallow or as deep as 90 feet (27 m).

Oysters' gills not only enable them to get oxygen from the water but also serve as food carriers and for some, as places to carry young oysters. The gills are folds of the body which extend into a cavity through which water can flow freely. Little hairlike bodies on the inside of the tube fan the water to the gills. After oxygen is taken in by the gills and carbon dioxide is given off, the water is fanned out of the oyster's body through another tube.

The gills have a sticky covering which gathers tiny animals and plants from the water as the water currents flow by. This is how the oyster gets its food. About a gallon (3.8 l) of water goes through the gills of an oyster in an hour.

Another use for gills is shown by the European oyster, which hatches its eggs in its gills and carries the young there for the first few days. American oysters deposit their eggs directly into the sea where they hatch by themselves. Young oysters are so tiny that they look like specks in the water. They move about for a day or so, then settle down on something solid. There they attach themselves and stay for the rest of their lives. Many are eaten by other animals, but an oyster can live several years and females lay millions of eggs, so there are many oysters left to grow to the adult stage.

Oysters have natural enemies. Starfish are the worst. The starfish wraps itself around the oyster, attaches its tubelike feet to both halves of the shell, and begins to pull. When some of its tube-feet tire, others do the work. Eventually, the oyster tires and its shell opens. The starfish can then eat the soft body. Another enemy is a little snail that bores through the oyster's shell and sucks out the soft part.

Oyster

Perhaps the biggest threat to oysters is the fact that people like to eat them. Raising oysters has become an important industry and there are many beds where the oysters are raised for food. Oyster farmers scatter shells in shallow water to provide places for the baby oysters to attach themselves.

Another oyster, related to the edible oyster, is also raised in beds, not for food, but for pearls. Sometimes the water carries a grain of sand or some other bit of hard material between the hinged shells of the oyster. The animal has no way of getting the sand out and its body is irritated by the small object. It gradually covers the grain with a heavy coating which is like the inside lining of its shell. Soon a second coat is formed on top of the first one. In time, the grain of sand gets many coats of the shiny shell-like covering. These coverings make a beautiful and valuable pearl. Only pearl oysters can make pearls of a quality good enough to be used in jewelry.

Starfish

Invertebrates with Spiny Skins

The oyster's enemy, the starfish, has a name that isn't very accurate because the little animal isn't a fish. It belongs to a group of spiny-skinned invertebrates. This scratchy skin is the starfish's best protection from enemies.

Like other animals of its kind, the starfish has a system of many water-filled tubes in its body. Tube feet extend out from the water tubes on the underside of the starfish's arms. The starfish uses its tube feet to move about and to catch its food. Since it has no head or tail, a starfish can move in any direction. The animals do most of their moving by night. During the daytime they rest hidden among rocks or burrow in the sand until they are almost covered.

Suction cups on the ends of its feet make it possible for the starfish to walk over slippery rocks. A starfish can also turn itself over using its tube feet. Although starfish have gills with which to breathe, the walls of their tube feet are also important because oxygen and carbon dioxide pass in and out through them. If a starfish loses one of its arms, it can grow another. A badly injured starfish can often recover in this way.

Female starfish may lay thousands of eggs, although many will never hatch because they become food for other animals. Baby starfish don't have arms and look quite different from their parents. When they are first hatched, they swim around near the surface of the ocean for a few days before they settle to the bottom where they will live.

Starfish are often brightly colored and not all of them have five arms. Sea urchins, sand dollars, and sea cucumbers are relatives of the starfish and are part of the same group of spiny-skinned invertebrates. They can also grow new body parts if some are lost in an accident. If you spend time on the seashore, you may find many of these spiny-skinned animals left behind by a changing tide.

Sea urchin

Brian Parker/TOM STACK & ASSOCIATES

Sponge

Swimming Skeletons

If you use a sponge to clean off a sink top, you probably have a product made of plastic. These plastic sponges are imitations of an animal that has been used for years for washing almost everything— from the human body to the windows in the house. These real sponges are large, tan, and absorbent. They are the skeletons of sea creatures.

For centuries people knew about the sponges and used them frequently. But they thought these strange objects that seemed to grow from the bottom of the sea were plants. Then for a while, they thought they were part plant and part animal. More modern scientists finally learned how sponges breathe and get food; then they knew that these creatures are animals.

The sponge gets its shape from its skeleton, the small openings of which are filled with a jellylike substance when the sponge is living. The skeleton holds the jellylike mass together and keeps it from collapsing. This mass contained in the skeleton is very active. It swallows many gallons of water a day, taking the air and tiny animals from it. Then it spouts the water out again like a fountain. The larger tubes, or canals, are lined with very tiny hairlike paddles that push the water through the sponge, much as water is pushed through the tubes of an oyster.

There are many kinds of sponges. Some are small and soft, and others hard and as big as a barrel. They grow in many shapes and colors. Although most of them grow in the salt water of the ocean, a few kinds live in fresh water or streams. One interesting kind of sponge is called the finger sponge because each branch is about six inches (15 cm) long and shaped like a finger. The most beautiful sponge, which grows about a foot (30 cm) tall and is shaped like a tube, is called "Venus's flower basket." The skeleton of this strange sponge looks like silver-colored glass.

The only sponges of economic importance are the ordinary sponges that people often use for baths and for house cleaning. These have been found in great numbers in the Mediterranean Sea and off the coasts of Florida and the Bahama Islands. Tarpon Springs, on the west coast of Florida, is a leading center of the sponge industry.

Sponges are usually gathered from the bottom of the oceans by deep sea divers, but sometimes they are snagged in shallow water by long-handled hooks which sponge fishermen carry in their boats. Live sponges look a little like beef liver when they are first taken from the water. They are hung in the sun until the jellylike mass inside the skeleton begins to dry. Then they are pounded and washed and dried again.

Sponges can produce young sponges in more than one way. The female sponge may grow bumps, or *buds*, on her body, which break off to form new sponges. She also lays eggs which will hatch into young sponges. After they hatch, they swim about for a time, then attach themselves to something solid at the bottom of the ocean. In addition, if a sponge is cut into several pieces, each piece may grow into a new sponge.

Most animals won't eat sponges because of their unpleasant taste and smell. One crab, called a sponge crab, wears a sponge on its back. Then it won't be attacked by other animals.

Sponges have become less common in recent years because of disease, overharvesting, and changes in their habitat.

Periiwinkles

Invertebrates with One Shell

Almost everyone has seen some kind of snail. There are big, little, and medium-sized snails. They live in ponds, oceans, and gardens. They move slowly, no matter how big they are, and they carry their houses, or shells, with them. This shell is actually the snail's skeleton. A snail has only one foot, but that foot is a big part of its body.

Some snails eat plants. Other snails eat animals. Some snails breathe with gills. Other snails have lungs.

One kind of snail lives in freshwater ponds. It is called a tadpole snail because of its shape. This snail has lungs, so although it finds food at the bottom of a pond, it must come to the surface to breathe. This snail builds a slimy thread of material that forms a ladder to the water's surface. The snail climbs the ladder, then drops to the bottom when it is ready. The tadpole snail lays many eggs in a jellylike mass. When the young snails first hatch, their shells are very delicate. They eat a great deal and as they grow, their shells harden and are soon ready to protect their soft bodies.

Another snail, the periwinkle, lives in salt water. Its shell, about the size of a person's thumbnail, is often yellowish or greenish brown in color. The periwinkle is often found on rocks and seaweed along the shores of the Atlantic Ocean.

A much larger snail is the queen conch. It may be more than one foot (30 cm) long. Its body is used for food in some countries.

The land snail, often seen in gardens, lays a path as it travels. The underside of its foot gives off a slimy substance as it moves, and the snail leaves a thin layer of this substance behind. If the weather becomes very dry, the garden snail pulls its foot inside its shell and seals up the opening with a layer of the slimy material. In this way, the snail's body is protected from drying up. In winter, land snails dig down into the ground, seal themselves in their shells, and sleep until spring.

Land snails have two pairs of tentacles to help them feel their way. The longer pair has an eye at the end of each tentacle.

One kind of land snail is used as food. These snails are raised on farms and are fed vegetables. Snails can eat such food because they have hundreds of sharp teeth on their tongues.

Snail

Brian Parker/TOM STACK & ASSOCIATES

OTHER INVERTEBRATES

Insects

No matter where you live, you have seen insects. These are usually very small animals and many of them have wings. Some live in fields, some in trees, and some in houses and other buildings.

Every insect has three parts to its body. These are the head, the thorax, and the abdomen. Every insect has six legs and two antennae. If a small creature doesn't match this description, it isn't an insect.

Most insects have one large eye on each side of the head. This eye is made up of many tiny lenses. It is called a *compound eye*. Some insects, such as grasshoppers, have more than two eyes; they have both compound eyes and *simple eyes*, or eyes with just one lens.

Most insects also have wings, usually two pairs. These wings are attached to the insect's thorax. Some insects—flies, for example—have just one pair of wings. Others, such as worker ants, have no wings at all. Many insects are pests; some carry disease. Insects are important members of the animal kingdom.

Social Insects

Ant colony

Some very common insects live in groups or communities. These insects are called *social insects*. Ants are social insects. They live and work together in colonies.

There are thousands of different kinds of ants in the world, but the black ant, found everywhere north of the equator, is probably one of the most common. When you see a hole in the ground with a mound of earth around it, stop and look carefully. The hole may be the entrance of a black ant colony, for these ants build their nests under the ground.

The hole leads down into a tunnel that branches off in many directions, making a network of tunnels. At some places, the tunnels widen to make rooms. The ants use these rooms for different purposes. Some are storerooms; some are ant nurseries.

How does an ant colony begin? Queen ants and male ants are born with thin wings somewhat like those of bees. As soon as a young queen ant is strong enough, she flies away from her home. A young male flies with her and they mate in the air. This is the only flight the ants make. Soon after they land, the queen tears off her wings and the male ant dies.

The queen will start a colony by digging a small tunnel under a stone or clump of roots. At the end of the tunnel, she builds a room. It may take several days of hard work to make the room and the queen becomes very tired. When the room is finished, she closes its opening. For a while the queen ant rests. Then she begins to lay tiny oval eggs. After a few days, the eggs hatch into larvae, which the queen feeds with a liquid from her body. The larvae grow and spin cocoons around themselves in the *pupa* stage. When the insects come out of their cocoons, they are full-grown ants.

The first ants will be worker ants and they will find food for the queen and dig tunnels and rooms, making a new ant colony. The queen won't do any more work; her only purpose now is to lay eggs.

Some of the worker ants in each ant colony are caretaker ants called nurses. The nurses care for the ant eggs. These eggs are sticky on the outside. The nurses gather the eggs into small balls they can carry from room to room. The nurses see that the eggs are kept warm so that they will hatch. If one room seems too cold, the nurses move the eggs to a warmer one. On sunny days, the eggs are usually kept in a room near the surface. After dark, these rooms lose the sun's warmth and the egg balls may be moved deeper in the ant colony. As soon as the eggs are hatched, the tiny larvae are fed a fluid from the nurses' bodies.

After the larvae have been fed several times, they make cocoons and pass into the pupa stage. The largest cocoons hold the queens. The workers carry the cocoons from room to room just as they did the eggs. Sometimes they are carried up and placed under a stone or board where it is warm. The ants won't go off and leave the pupae. They will always protect the young ants.

Even after the pupae are full-grown and have left their cocoons, the ants feed them until they are able to care for themselves. As soon as

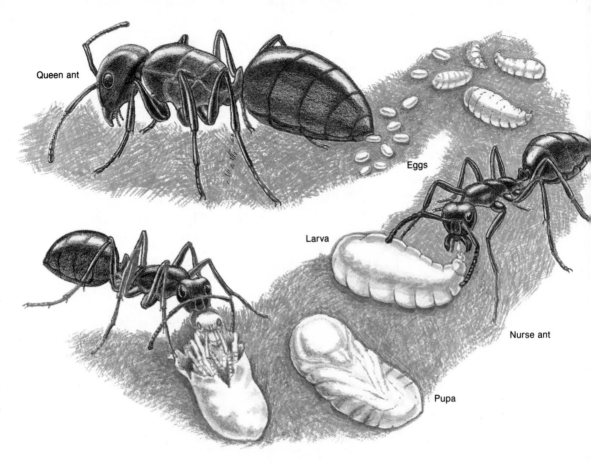

Queen ant

Eggs

Larva

Nurse ant

Pupa

they are able, the young queens and males make their flight and the workers, which have no wings, begin their duties, tunneling out new rooms, nursing, or finding food.

Worker ants can't see well, but they do well in finding food. They can both feel and smell with their antennae. As the workers run busily back and forth getting food for the colony, they often stop to touch the feelers of other ants, just as though they might be exchanging a message. Ants have extremely strong jaws. Sometimes they bring back foods, such as large seeds, that are bigger than they are. Then other workers help them drag the food inside.

The black ants don't live only on the solid foods which the workers bring in; they also keep plant lice, or aphids, which furnish them with a plant liquid called honeydew. The aphids suck juices from plants and give off sugar and water. When an ant rubs an aphid with its antennae, the aphid gives out drops of honeydew. In winter, the ants carry the aphids to underground rooms. In spring, they carry them back to the green plants that are beginning to grow.

In the neighborhood of the black ant colony there may be soldier ants. These ants may rob the black ant colony of its pupae. The black ants will try to move the pupae to safety, but some may be stolen. Then the soldier ants carry the pupae to their own colony. Here they may be used as food, or they may be raised to be workers in the new colony. Because of this, you may sometimes see black ants working in a soldier ant colony.

The black ant colony will continue to grow. Ants may live for many years in the same place, constantly enlarging their home. The mound of dirt by its entrance grows larger as new tunnels and rooms are dug. If the anthill is in a yard, it spoils the lawn. Some ants may find their way into homes. When the insects become pests, people usually try to destroy the ants, but it is difficult to get rid of the thousands and thousands of ants in a colony. The ants that survive will always begin a new colony.

Besides black ants, there are many other kinds of ants. Yellow ants may be seen looking for sugar. Tailor ants use silklike thread from cocoons to mend their homes. Leaf-cutting ants strip leaves from a tree and carry them back to their nests by holding the leaves over their heads. Because of this, people sometimes call them parasol ants. Leaf-cutting ants chew up the leaves and use the pulp to fertilize mushroom or fungus gardens in their underground rooms. These ants eat only mushrooms.

The Australian bulldog ant is one of the biggest ants and is a fierce fighter. Carpenter ants burrow into logs. Termites, which are often called white ants, eat through wood. They are really relatives of cockroaches, however, and aren't ants.

In both Africa and South America, there are army ants which will attack any animal they can catch. These fierce ants line up and march along, eating whatever is in their way. They have no home but carry their queen and young ants along. Sometimes the whole army gathers and forms an enormous ball, with the queen and the babies in the center. When army ants are on the march, even a large animal may be eaten if it doesn't get out of the way.

Another common social insect is the honeybee. A honeybee family usually consists of at least several thousand bees and there may be as

Honeybee

many as 50,000. In all of these there is one queen bee and perhaps about 100 males, or *drones*. The rest are worker bees.

Like other insects, honeybees have six legs and three body parts. They have two pairs of strong wings and five eyes, two of which are compound. In growing up, bees go through the same stages many insects do—egg, larva, pupa, and adult.

Queens, drones, and workers don't look alike. A queen bee has a long pointed body. All she does is lay eggs in the comb cells which the workers have prepared. Her body shape enables her to place the eggs deep in the cells.

Drones are large and plump. Although they don't work, they are important, for one of them will mate with the queen. Bees mate in the air, and soon after it has mated, the drone dies. The queen bee then returns to the hive to lay eggs.

Honeycomb cells

Worker bees are smaller than either the queen or drones, but they do all of the work. They clean the hive and store up food for winter. On their back legs they have baskets in which *pollen*—the dustlike substance which comes from the center of certain flowers—is packed and carried. They also have stiff, wiry spines with which they remove the pollen from the baskets. On their front legs are wax pinchers which the bees use in building the honeycomb.

A queen bee lays two kinds of eggs. The eggs she lays in the drone cells hatch into drones. The rest of her eggs become either workers or queens. These are the same kind of larvae at first—tiny white grubs that look nothing like bees. Whether they will grow into queens or workers depends on the way they are fed.

For the first three days, the worker-bee grubs are fed bee jelly, a whitish substance spit up by the workers. For the next three days nectar and pollen from flowers are added. Then the workers' cells are covered over. The grubs wrap themselves in a heavy coating and go into their pupa stage for about two weeks. After that time the insects emerge from their cells as full-grown worker bees.

Some of the grubs are fed bee jelly for six days instead of three, and these grow into queens instead of workers. It is easy to tell which cells have the baby queens in them because the workers have made these cells larger.

Before a new queen hatches, the old queen leaves to find a new home, taking most of her old workers with her to begin a new hive. This keeps the number of bees in the old hive from becoming too large. When the first of the new queens hatches, she looks for other queen cells, tears them open, and kills the young queens inside. If two queens hatch at the same time, one will usually sting the other to death. Each hive can have only one queen. The surviving new queen mates and begins to lay eggs.

When the young worker bees first come out of their cells, they gorge on honey which the older bees have made from the nectar of flowers. Their wings are not yet strong enough for them to fly out for pollen and nectar. Their first task is to provide wax for the comb builders. Quietly they cling to the inside of the hive while wax seeps out of wax pockets on their abdomens. Small balls of the wax are pinched off by the comb builders.

Some of the young bees become comb builders, too. Others become nurses, housekeepers, food gatherers, or guards. Some bees help heat and ventilate the hive. On cool days, some worker bees form a blanket over the brood cells to help keep the babies warm. Workers stationed near the slitlike entrance of the hive provide the ventilating system by fanning their wings rapidly. This forces fresh air through the hive. It is good exercise for the worker bees that will soon be carrying pollen and nectar, for they must begin to gather this food as soon as their wings are strong enough. When a worker leaves the hive to collect pollen and nectar, it may need to hunt to find the right flowers, but when it goes back to the hive, it flies in the shortest and most direct line.

Some worker bees serve as guards for the hive and sniff at every bee that enters, for bees from other hives aren't allowed inside. If the wrong kind of bee should get into a honeybee hive, the guards will chase it out.

While the young bees and some of the old workers continue to develop their hive, the old queen and her workers have found a new home. When a bee family goes out looking for a place for a hive, it is said to be *swarming*. Many of the workers cling together, making a large conelike formation about the queen. Other workers search carefully for a good place, which may be in a hollow tree, or perhaps in a new hive which a beekeeper has set out. As soon as the queen has moved into the hive, the other bees will follow. The workers start at once making brood cells and the queen begins to lay eggs.

Next, some of the worker bees will begin to gather food. A bee family works on only one kind of flower at a time. For example, when a bee family is making clover honey, the bees of that hive visit only clover flowers. Later on, when making buckwheat honey, they visit only buckwheat flowers. This process helps the plants on which they work. The pollen the bees carry goes to other plants of the same kind where it is needed. Many plants won't produce seeds unless pollen from the same kind of plant is brought to them by the wind, or by birds or bees. So bees are important in pollinating plants as well as in producing honey.

Keeping bees is a profitable business for people willing to collect the honey made by bees. A beekeeper may construct hives and place them where bees can find nectar and pollen. When a beekeeper sees a swarm beginning, he or she may brush the bees into a new hive. If the queen can be placed in the hive, the others will follow.

Inside a beehive, the bees will build the comb which holds the honey. Each cell in a honeycomb has six sides. The cell walls are so thin that if you laid 350 walls side by side, they would be only about an inch (2.5 cm) thick. The cells are used for both egg-laying and storage of honey, which is made when nectar from flowers is mixed with the juice in the worker bees' mouths. All summer the worker bees gather food. They pack their pollen baskets and suck nectar from flowers. When they return to the hive, the honey is deposited in cells.

By fall, each hive has a good supply of honey, more than enough to last it all winter. However, only certain members of the hive are allowed to live once summer ends. All drones are stung to death and any workers that are no longer useful are cast out from the hive. Only the queen bee and the strong workers will prepare for winter. When the weather first turns cold, the bees arrange themselves in the form of a hollow ball which makes it easier for them to keep warm. This ball of bees will hang from a layer of honeycomb so that their winter supply of food is close to them.

It is from this winter food supply that beekeepers gather honey to sell. When the comb is cleaned, the wax from which it has been made can also be sold. Some kinds of candles are made of beeswax.

Bees and their relatives, the wasps, live in most parts of the world. Besides the honeybee, the bumblebee, a larger insect with a loud buzz, is common in some areas.

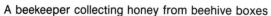
A beekeeper collecting honey from beehive boxes

Jumping Insects

Have you ever watched a track meet that included the long jump? About how far would you expect an athlete who is six feet (1.8 m) tall to jump? A very good jumper might jump three or four times his or her height—maybe 25 feet (7.5 m). The insect we call the grasshopper can't jump 25 feet, but it can and often does jump 20 times its own length. That same ability for the human jumper would result in an amazing leap of as much as 120 feet (36 m).

It is the grasshopper's long, strong hind legs that enable it to jump so far. Like other insects, a grasshopper has six legs, which it uses well in walking. Because of a sticky substance on its feet, it can even walk straight up a smooth wall.

Besides being able to jump amazing distances, this insect is also a good flier and does much of its traveling by flying. Most grasshoppers have four wings, two of which are stiff and serve as covers for the other two. When they aren't in use, a grasshopper's wings are folded back against its body.

A grasshopper has many eyes and can see in all directions at once. On each side of its head there is a big compound eye, made up of many six-sided eyes. There is also a small simple eye in front of each compound eye and another in the middle of the insect's head. With so many eyes, the grasshopper can watch for enemies in all directions, even though it can't turn its head from side to side as many insects are able to do.

There are two well-known types of grasshoppers. The long-horned, or meadow, grasshopper has fine, wavy antennae that are longer than its body. It lives on the ground. This grasshopper has a relative that lives in trees. It is called a katydid. The short-horned grasshopper is sometimes called a locust. It has short, stiff antennae.

Grasshoppers like to eat grass. They cling to the blades of grass as they eat, holding them in an up-and-down position with little claws, or fingers, at the sides of their mouths. The grass is cut by the sharp edges of their jaws. The upper lips of a grasshopper are notched in the middle. The jaws close together from the sides. They enable the grasshopper to cut and chew food. The jaws can give a hard pinch that you would feel if the grasshopper closed them on your finger.

To protect themselves from other insects, grasshoppers spit out a brown liquid, which has an unpleasant odor. It also helps them digest their food.

Although a grasshopper has no skeleton on the inside of its body, it has a smooth, shiny, firm coating on the outside which serves as protection. The grasshopper has an unusual way of breathing: air is taken in through tiny openings, smaller than pinholes, in its abdomen.

The short-horned grasshopper also has ears on its abdomen. These ears are round pieces of tissue that are protected by the wings of the insect when the wings are folded back. Have you ever heard a grasshopper "sing"? Male grasshoppers make a grating noise by rubbing their hind legs against the edges of their stiff wings.

Long-horned grasshoppers and their relatives, the katydids, have ears on their first pair of legs, just below the first joint. The male grasshoppers and katydids make a noise, or "sing," by rubbing their wings together. They attract the females with this noise. Females make no sound.

When a female grasshopper is ready to lay eggs, she makes a hole about an inch (2.5 cm) deep in the ground. There she lays masses of eggs which are held together by a sticky substance. The eggs are usually laid in fall and hatched in spring. Young grasshoppers, called *nymphs*, have no wings. The wings begin to develop as the insects grow. Since grasshoppers have an external skeleton, they must shed this hard covering several times as they grow larger.

Both long-horned and short-horned grasshoppers eat leaves and stems of plants but don't usually cause severe crop damage. Occasionally, however, the short-horned grasshopper swarms in huge numbers and can destroy a whole field of grain. One type of grasshopper, the desert locust, frequently causes enormous destruction in Africa. A shortage of food and an overpopulation of the insects may cause them to swarm and migrate, eating everything along their path.

A swarm of locusts

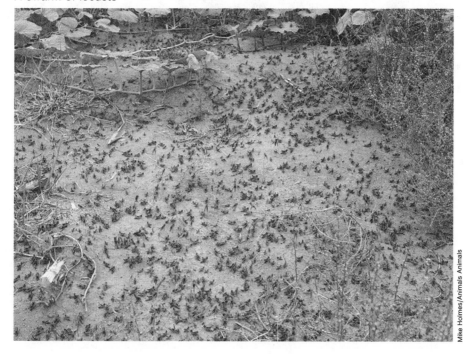

Mike Holmes/Animals Animals

Insects with Scaly Wings

An interesting long-distance traveler is the beautiful insect called the monarch butterfly. Like all butterflies and moths, the monarch has wings which seem to be covered with powder. However, when placed under a microscope, the "powder" is shown instead to be tiny scales. These scales, which give the wings their color, are arranged in an orderly way. Because they have scales on their wings, butterflies and moths belong to a special group of insects called *scale wings.*

In early summer, a monarch butterfly will search for milkweed plants. The insect lays several eggs on the underside of the milkweed leaves. After several days these eggs hatch into larvae—tiny black-and-white caterpillars. These begin to move about on the milkweed plant, eating the leaves day and night until they are so big they must shed their skins. This shedding is called *molting*.

The caterpillars molt several times. After about two weeks they have become large caterpillars with green, yellow, and black stripes. Soon each caterpillar will crawl under a milkweed leaf and spin a pad of silk. It fastens itself to this pad. Hanging head down, the caterpillar will molt once more. This time, however, it won't grow a new skin. Instead, it makes itself a green bag with gold-and-black trimming. Now it is in its pupa stage. The green bag is called a *chrysalis*.

Eventually, the green bag turns bluish-black and begins to move. Finally, an orange-brown butterfly with six feet and four wings emerges from the bag. At first, its wings look wet and wrinkled, but the butterfly begins to fan them and soon they are dry and bright. The tiny caterpillar has become the full-grown insect known as a monarch butterfly.

Monarch butterflies have long tubelike tongues which they use to suck nectar from flowers. They also have antennae with knobs on the ends. Because they travel from flower to flower, butterflies are important; like bees, they help pollinate plants by carrying pollen from one flower to another. They can do little harm. Birds ordinarily won't eat a monarch butterfly. The milkweed that the caterpillars ate makes the butterflies taste unpleasant. Their bright colors may warn the birds to avoid this insect. But lizards, wasps, beetles, and certain mammals will eat the butterfly.

In North America, adult monarch butterflies often migrate, although most of their butterfly and moth relatives don't. In the fall hundreds of these colorful insects may gather and begin their trip south. As the sun goes down, they will land in trees. Here they hang from the branches, looking like rows of yellow-orange leaves. Thousands of these butter-flies spend the winter in southern California or near Mexico City. In the spring, they travel north again and some of them even reach southern Canada by late summer. Scientists don't know how these delicate insects can fly such distances or how they find their way from one part of the continent to another.

A moth is another insect with scales on its wings. However, moths and butterflies are different in some ways. The bodies of moths are usually larger and not as slender as those of butterflies. Most moths have feathery antennae instead of straight antennae with knobs on the ends. They do most of their flying at night, while butterflies fly in the daytime. When butterflies alight, they hold their wings straight up over their backs. Most moths hold their wings spread out or directed backward along their sides.

Moth caterpillars found in several places throughout the world are incorrectly called silkworms; they are not worms. The cecropia moth is one of the largest silkworm moths, often five inches (12.5 cm) from the edge of one wing to the edge of the other.

A cecropia moth will lay many small cream-colored eggs on the leaf of a fruit tree. The eggs will hatch into tiny caterpillars which will begin to eat the leaves. After about four days, the caterpillars will molt and grow new skins. This happens several times and each new skin is a different color. By the time the caterpillars molt for the fourth time, they are about three inches (7.5 cm) long.

Soon the caterpillars will begin to spin cocoons, winding long silk threads around their bodies. This silk comes from the caterpillar's mouth and is made inside its body. On the outside, these cocoons look much like brown paper. The moths are in the pupa stage. In spring, the moths, wet and crumpled, crawl out of their cocoons, fan their wings, and fly off in search of a place to lay their eggs. These moths live for a few days on the food they stored while they were larvae. Then the moths die. They don't migrate like their monarch relatives.

One kind of silkworm moth has been raised in China for centuries because of the cocoons it spins. Soon after a cocoon is formed, it can be gathered and processed into silk thread. Silk thread, when woven into cloth, makes an expensive and beautiful material. Closely related to the cecropia moth, the Chinese silkworm moth is raised only for producing silk; it doesn't exist in the wild.

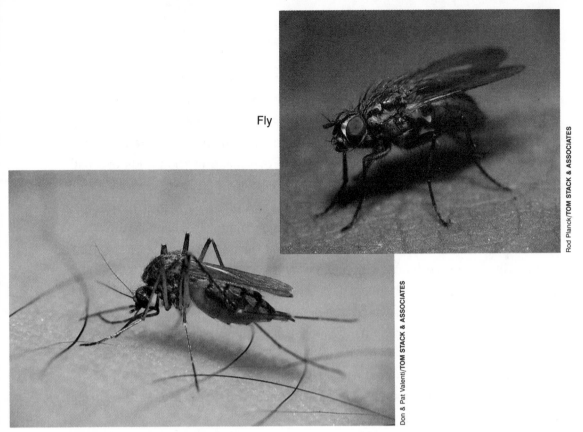

Fly

Mosquito

Insect Pests

You know that an animal pest is an animal that is in the wrong place or that has overpopulated. There are two insects, however, that most people think are always pests—houseflies and mosquitoes. Both insects are generally unpopular. It is hard to think of anything good that either of these insects does. Both of them grow from eggs to adults in such a short time that many generations live in a single season.

Flies and mosquitoes are alike in that they have only two wings, but, like other insects, they have six legs and three body parts—head, thorax, and abdomen. Their legs and wings are fastened to the thorax.

There are many kinds of flies, and some of them are helpful because they pollinate flowers. Other flies eat harmful insects. The housefly, however, is a dangerous pest. It lives all over the world, wherever people live, for the garbage that people leave helps these flies to breed.

Although the fly has no nose, it can detect odors a long distance away; its antennae act as smellers. Instead of a mouth, a fly has a small trunk, or proboscis, with which it sucks up its food.

A fly's head is almost all eyes so the fly can see in all directions. On each side of its head is a compound eye made of thousands of small eyes. These eyes are part of its protection.

A female housefly lays many eggs in manure piles or garbage dumps. These filthy places are perfect breeding grounds because the fly larvae depend on this material for their food during the first week of their lives. Larvae hatch within a few hours after the eggs are laid. They grow fast and in about six days they get brown coats, which make them look like grains of wheat. Their pupa stage lasts about five days. The adult flies develop from the pupae and they never grow any larger. Adult flies live about three weeks.

Since flies lay so many eggs and it takes less than two weeks for a fly to reach its adult stage, it is easy to understand why there are so many flies in the world.

Mosquitoes are equally annoying insects. Like flies, they go through four stages while growing up and their life cycle is also very short. A typical mosquito will lay eggs on the surface of water. The eggs stick together and float. For a few days the larvae that hatch remain in the water. They are tiny wriggling things hanging below the surface of the water. Then they become pupae, often called tumblers. In about five more days, they are adult mosquitoes.

Male mosquitoes live on plant juices. They have no sharp mouth parts. Female mosquitoes, however, suck blood whenever they can. Their sucking tubes have sharp points like needles with which they puncture the skin of a victim.

All mosquito bites can cause infection because they itch and cause the victim to scratch. Some mosquitoes, however, may carry disease from one person to another. A mosquito that stands on its head when it bites is called the Anopheles mosquito. It is found mostly in tropical regions. This mosquito can transmit malaria if it first bites a person with the disease and then bites other people.

The Aedes is a mosquito that carries yellow fever. It also lives in very warm climates.

There are few safe ways to destroy these two insects. Chemicals are sometimes used to kill them. It isn't wise, however, to use large amounts of chemicals or to use them near people or water sources. In general, chemicals are avoided. Some people tried putting oil on the water where mosquitoes bred, but the result was to kill many helpful water animals.

There are two safe ways to control mosquitoes and flies. One way is to destroy their habitats when possible. If flies breed best in garbage, they can be controlled if garbage isn't left uncovered. If mosquitoes breed on the surface of still water, puddles, ditches, and other standing water can be drained or dried up.

The second way is for us to do all we can to save the birds, bats, dragonflies, and fish that eat these insects. Each of these animals can rid us of hundreds of mosquitoes and flies every day.

ARACHNIDS

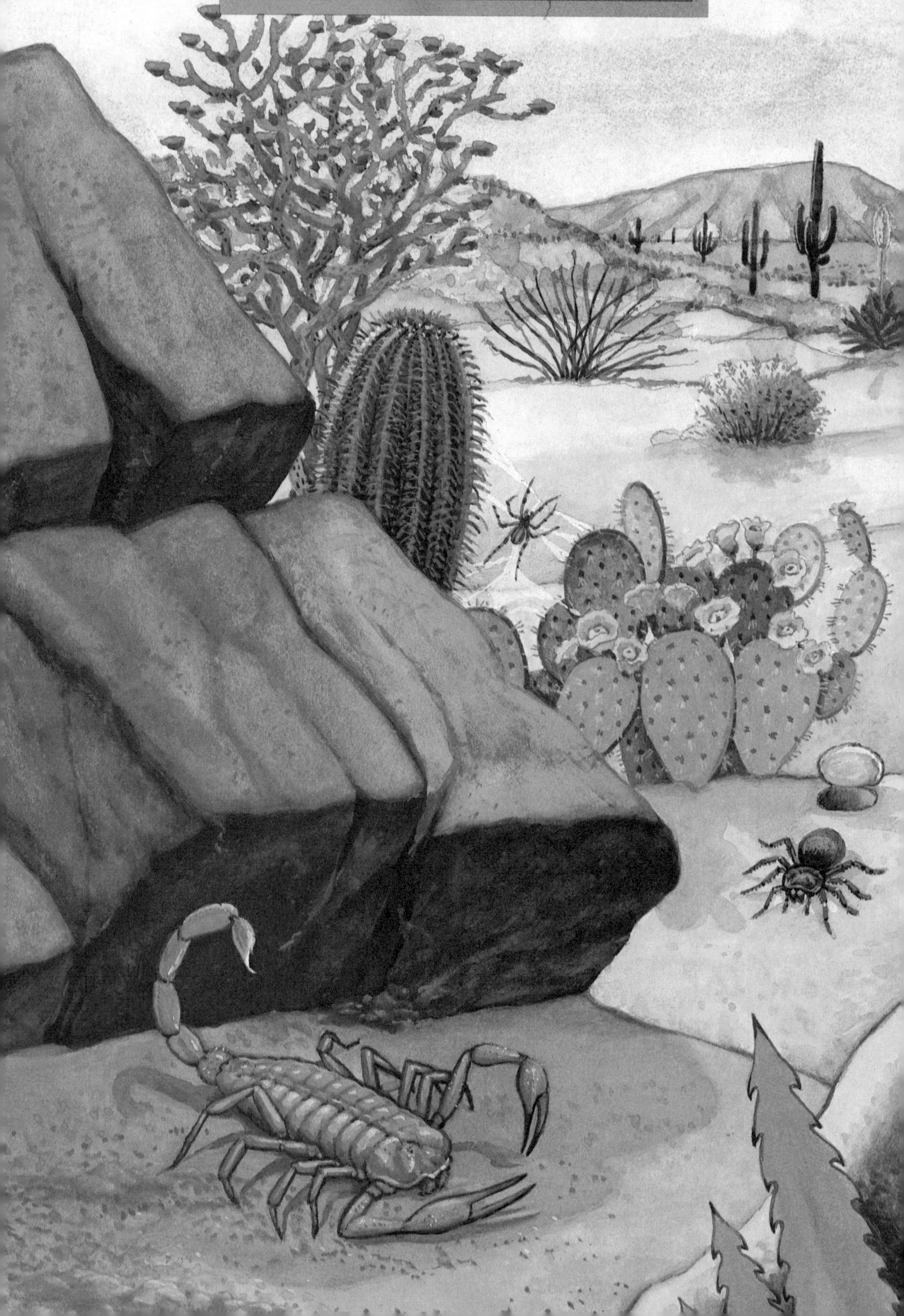

When scientists give names to animals, they usually use Latin words that tell something about the animal. The word *insect*, for example, comes from a Latin word that means "to cut," because an insect's body is cut or divided into three parts. However, when scientists were giving a name to a small animal that has eight legs and spins a web, they didn't use a Latin word; they named it after a woman in a very old Greek story.

Thousands of years ago, Greek storytellers told about a woman named Arachne who could weave the most beautiful cloth in the world. She became very proud of this and bragged to everyone. Arachne made a serious mistake. The goddess Athena was also a weaver and when

Arachne bragged to the goddess that she was a better weaver, Athena challenged her to a contest. Of course, Athena won. As a punishment, the goddess turned Arachne into a tiny animal that must spend its life weaving. Arachne became a spider. The scientific name for spiders and their relatives, ticks and mites, is *arachnid*.

Arachnids are small invertebrates often confused with insects, but arachnids have only two body parts and eight legs. In spite of the story of Arachne, not all arachnids weave webs.

One of the most common arachnids is the garden spider. This small creature is about one inch (2.5 cm) long and has a hard outer covering on its body. The female is black with spots of bright orange. The front part of her body is covered with silvery white hairs. This spider has eight eyes. Instead of jaws, it has fangs with which to poison insects. It breathes through two lung slits in the lower part of its abdomen. The male garden spider is smaller than the female and less brightly colored. Like a drone in the bee family, the male spider doesn't work. After it mates, it is usually eaten by the female.

In the fall, the female garden spider lays hundreds of eggs in a sac. During winter, when food is scarce, the female dies. The eggs in their waterproof sac remain on a plant and the baby spiders hatch inside the nest. There the strong ones survive by eating the weak ones. When it is warm enough outside, the surviving spiders come out of the sac. They grow fast and their hard outer coverings are shed many times as they get larger. The young female spiders will find a branch or twig and begin to lay a trap for their much-needed food.

With her hind legs, the female spider draws silk from the glands in her abdomen. She fastens this silk thread to a branch. As the thread gets longer, she lets herself down by it. With the help of a breeze, she is soon able to swing herself across to a nearby plant. There she fastens the other end of the thread. Now she has a bridge and the beginning of a web.

The spider spins other threads that cross the first and fastens the ends to other branches. Finally she has a framework that looks like the rim and spokes of a wheel. The threads are stretched tight and fastened where they cross. Then the spider begins at the center and spins a new thread, going around and around in toward the center. This thread is sticky and quite closely woven. The old threads are cut away as the new sticky threads are put in. At last, after the spider has spun more threads across the front and back of the web, it is finished. It takes a garden spider about an hour to spin this kind of web, which is called an orb-web.

Now the spider moves to the center of the web and waits. Soon a fly strikes the web. It struggles, but the sticky threads hold it fast. Quickly the spider bites the fly with her two poison fangs and paralyzes it. She sucks out the liquid part of the fly's body. Then she cuts away part of the web to let the rest of the body fall. Carefully she mends the web and waits for another insect to be caught.

The thousands of kinds of spiders spin different kinds of webs. The grass spider makes a funnel-shaped web. The house spider weaves a web called a cobweb. The jumping spider climbs to the top of a plant. Her silk spinners float upward, and a breeze carries her through the air. The trapdoor spider digs a little tube in the ground and weaves a round door over it. When she is hungry, she hides under the door until she feels the quiver of an insect passing. Then she pops open the door and pulls the insect inside. The tarantula, which is hairy and may be three or four inches (8-10 cm) long, hunts for its food, chasing lizards, insects, and sometimes even baby birds.

Some spiders don't put their egg sacs on a plant but carry them on their bodies. When the baby spiders hatch, they ride around on the mother's back until they are able to find food.

Spiders have several enemies, but the wasp is the worst one. A female wasp may sting a spider, paralyzing it. Then she lays eggs on the spider's body so the newly hatched wasp babies will have a source of food. Many birds also eat spiders.

Although spiders poison the insects they eat, their bites are usually harmless to human beings. Very few have a poison that will hurt people. The black widow spider, about a half inch (1.25 cm) long, is poisonous to humans. It has a shiny black body with a red hourglass-shaped spot on its underside. There is a brown house spider that is also poisonous. Most spiders, however, are of great help to people because they eat thousands of insects that would otherwise damage crops and garden plants.

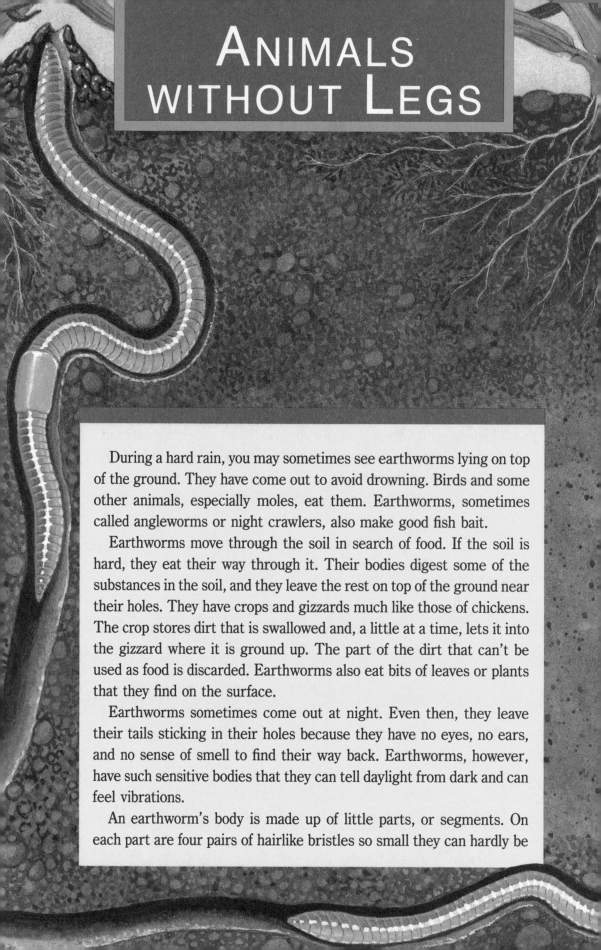

ANIMALS WITHOUT LEGS

During a hard rain, you may sometimes see earthworms lying on top of the ground. They have come out to avoid drowning. Birds and some other animals, especially moles, eat them. Earthworms, sometimes called angleworms or night crawlers, also make good fish bait.

Earthworms move through the soil in search of food. If the soil is hard, they eat their way through it. Their bodies digest some of the substances in the soil, and they leave the rest on top of the ground near their holes. They have crops and gizzards much like those of chickens. The crop stores dirt that is swallowed and, a little at a time, lets it into the gizzard where it is ground up. The part of the dirt that can't be used as food is discarded. Earthworms also eat bits of leaves or plants that they find on the surface.

Earthworms sometimes come out at night. Even then, they leave their tails sticking in their holes because they have no eyes, no ears, and no sense of smell to find their way back. Earthworms, however, have such sensitive bodies that they can tell daylight from dark and can feel vibrations.

An earthworm's body is made up of little parts, or segments. On each part are four pairs of hairlike bristles so small they can hardly be

seen, but they help the worm crawl. An earthworm can grow a new head or tail if either is cut off, but it can't live if more than 10 of its front segments are removed.

Earthworms are soft, with no hard body parts. They drink and breathe through their skins, which must be kept moist. During dry spells, they burrow deeper to find damp earth. During cold or very dry weather, earthworms sometimes go as deep as eight feet (2.4 m). There a number of them may roll up together in a ball.

On a band about a third of the way back on the earthworm's body, a collarlike sac forms. This sac moves forward as the worm moves back, and the earthworm's eggs are collected in the sac. The cocoon that is formed in this way protects the small worms until they can survive on their own.

Earthworms are of great service to plants because grinding up the dirt makes it into better soil. Also, the worms bring to the surface particles of soil from lower levels, much as a gardener tries to do with tools. Through its tunnels, the earthworm helps air and water get into the earth. In hard ground, the roots of plants may even follow the worm holes. Earthworms also carry bits of vegetable material into the ground, which helps to enrich the soil. These little invertebrates deserve a high place on the list of most useful animals.

Plants
The Oldest Kingdom

You know that the animal kingdom is one of the best-known groups of living things. Another important and very large group is the kingdom of plants. Plants are like animals in that they live and grow, require food and water, and produce young like themselves. Of course, plants and animals are very different in some ways. The most obvious difference is that animals move about and plants don't. Another very important difference is that animals need plants for food. Green plants, on the other hand, can make their own food from substances in the soil and the water and from gases in the air. This process of making food is called *photosynthesis.*

In photosynthesis, carbon dioxide from the air enters the green plants through tiny openings in the leaves. Water enters through the roots and comes up through the stems. A green substance called *chlorophyll*, which gives the leaves their color, is in the cells of the plant. The chlorophyll causes the carbon dioxide and water to

Grazing cattle

manufacture sugar. The energy to do this is furnished by sunlight. The plants then use this sugar as food. Plants may change the sugar to another kind of food before they store it. For example, some plants make starch from the sugar and others make protein.

Which do you think have been in the world for a longer time, plants or animals? Why do you think this? If you consider the fact that all living things need food, you will know that the plant kingdom is older. All animals eat plants or eat other animals that eat plants. Therefore, animals couldn't exist without plants. Plants, on the other hand, don't eat animals, so some kinds of plants could have existed for a long time before there were any animals.

All forms of animal life depend upon green plants for food. We drink milk and eat eggs and meat. The cattle or goats that provide the milk and meat eat grass and grain, which are green plants. Eggs come from chickens that eat grain. Everything we eat, except salt and water, can be traced back to green plants. People can live without eating meat; they can't live without eating plants.

Members of the fungus kingdom also depend upon green plants for food. Without decaying green plants, fungi couldn't live. Green plants are *independent*. This means they make their own food. Nongreen fungi are *dependent*. They depend on other things for the food they need.

Scientists today can show that the plant kingdom is millions of years old. By a careful study of traces of plants left in the layers of rock in Earth's crust, scientists have been able to piece together much of the story. As is true of animals, the first plants were very small and lived in water. These plants must have been able to make their own food, as there was no other food for them. These first very simple plants were followed by larger green ones. Some of these may not have lived in water, but they would have needed much moisture. Liverworts and mosses, which we find growing today, are relatives of those plants of long ago.

Next came still larger plants—other mosses and ferns. Long ago, some of these were as large as trees are today. They are much smaller now. These plants grew their biggest during the Age of Amphibians and the Age of Reptiles millions of years ago. Plants that decayed and were buried during the Age of Amphibians helped to form the coal that is mined in our time.

Like animals, plants differ from one another in many ways. Many plants are very tiny. Other plants are enormous; some trees are nearly 300 feet (90 m) tall. Some plants live in water; others live in very dry climates. Some plants have seeds; others never have seeds. We eat parts of many plants, but other plants can't be eaten.

Like animals, plants are divided into two main groups and each group can be divided again. These two important groups of plants are plants with seeds and plants without seeds.

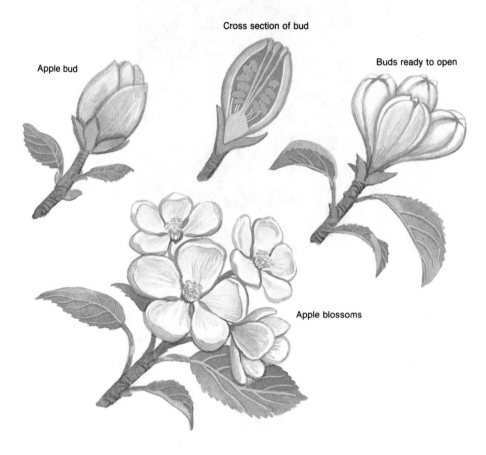

Cross section of bud

Apple bud

Buds ready to open

Apple blossoms

Plants with Seeds

Ferns may be among the oldest green plants, but no one has ever picked a bouquet of fern flowers. Ferns and mosses are among the many green plants that don't have flowers. These plants, and most water plants, are seedless. A flowering plant is always a seed plant and all seed plants have either flowers or cones.

Some flowering plants are small. Duckweed, which grows in lakes and ponds, is one of the smallest. Other flowering plants are large. Trees are the largest flowering plants.

Why do so many plants have flowers? People enjoy flowers because they are beautiful, because they make yards and parks look more attractive, and because many of them have a pleasant smell. But some flowers aren't pretty and many have no smell. Flowers don't exist for us to admire. Their purpose is to produce the seeds from which new plants will grow.

In all parts of the world, seed-bearing plants begin new life as new buds develop on shrubs and trees. You have probably looked at a swollen bud on a fruit tree. The bud is protected by a covering of tightly overlapping *sepals*, which look like tiny leaves. When the bud opens, the sepals separate and the petals unfold to form the flower. On most flowers, the petals are the most beautifully colored parts. Toward the center of the flower, you may see some threadlike stalks with little knobs on their tips. These are called *stamens* and it is within these knobs, or sacs, that pollen grains develop.

In the center of the flower, surrounded by the stamens, is the *pistil*. The lower part of the pistil is a bulb-shaped *ovary*. This is deep at the base of the flower. Within the ovary are tiny green balls, *ovules*. These ovules are the parts that will grow into seeds if fertilized by the pollen grains.

If you touch the knobs on the stamen of an apple blossom, you will find that the pollen on them is a fine yellow dust or powder that sticks to your finger. If you touch the upper, broadened part of the pistil, called a *stigma*, you will find that it is sticky. It is when the sticky stigma is covered by the powdery pollen from stamens that fertilization can occur.

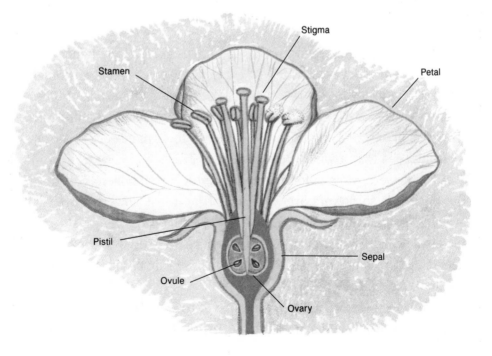

Violets

After pollen grains reach the stigma, they begin to take up moisture from the pistil. They swell and produce tiny tubes, which grow through the pistil until they reach the ovules. When one of these pollen tubes reaches an ovule, some of its contents enter the ovule and unite with the egg cell inside. Then the egg cell begins to form a seed. It is from this tiny seed that a whole new plant may grow.

A few flowers, violets, for example, use their own pollen to fertilize the pistil. These flowers are *self-pollinating*. Most flowers, however, are *cross-pollinated*. This means the pollen from one flower must reach the pistil of another flower in order to fertilize it. To do this, the flowers need help. Cross-pollination is important. It usually produces stronger and better plants.

In cross-pollination, nature sometimes provides special devices so that a flower won't be pollinated by its own pollen. In the plant called

Bloodroot

bloodroot, for instance, the pistil is ready to receive pollen before its own pollen is ripe. This means that bloodroot pistils have to depend upon insects to bring pollen from another bloodroot plant. Another plant, the geranium, works in just the opposite way. Here the pollen is ready before the pistils develop.

Another way that nature prevents self-pollination for some plants is to give some flowers only stamens and others only pistils. A cotton-wood tree is a good example of this kind of pollination.

Bees, flies, hummingbirds, butterflies, and moths are among the animals that help flowers to cross-pollinate. This is the reason that plants have bright or fragrant flowers—the plant has to attract its helpers.

You know that bees need the nectar from flowers to make honey in their hives. You know, too, that bees from one hive use nectar from one type of flower. This makes the bees very important helpers in cross-pollination.

When a bee settles on a flower, it is looking for food. If it has been to another flower, some of the pollen from that flower is on the bee's rear legs. As the bee searches for food, the pollen on its legs will stick to the pistil of the second flower. The fine fragrance from the flowers and their bright color have attracted the bee to the nectar and the bee has helped to pollinate the plant.

Since bees and butterflies work during the daytime, flowers that depend upon them for help are brightly colored and are more fragrant in daylight. Since moths work at night, flowers which depend on them are usually white, because white shows up best in the darkness. These flowers also usually have a strong scent, making it easier for the moths to find them.

Some flowers, like skunk cabbage, have an unpleasant odor that doesn't attract bees or butterflies. These flowers are often pollinated by flies.

Many plants depend upon one type of insect for cross-pollination. Many years ago, some people in Australia decided they wanted to grow a special kind of red clover from North America. Seeds were brought from the United States and planted. The plants grew very well and

produced fine flowers, but the flowers didn't produce seeds. The following year, more clover seeds were brought to Australia and another crop was planted. Again there were beautiful flowers but no seeds. Then someone discovered that the bumblebee is the insect that pollinates the red clover in the United States. There were no bumblebees in Australia and the bumblebee is the only insect with a tongue long enough to reach the nectar of the red clover flower. Colonies of bumblebees were brought to Australia to pollinate the red clover and it began to produce seeds.

Another interesting partnership exists between the yucca plant and the yucca moth. Neither could live without the other. The moth gathers pollen from the stamens of a yucca flower and rolls it into a ball. Then it goes to the flower of another yucca plant, deposits its eggs in the ovary, and climbs up to the stigma where it places the pollen. This, of course, fertilizes the ovules and they grow into seeds. When the moth eggs are hatched, the larvae eat about a third of the seeds. The others remain to produce more yucca plants. So the moth helps the yucca by pollinating it and the plant helps the moth by giving its young a home and its first food.

Yucca plant and yucca moth

Don & Esther Phillips/TOM STACK & ASSOCIATES

Dandelion seeds scattered by the wind

Do you think all seed-bearing plants are pollinated by insects? Nature uses other methods, too. Water is one of the agents that helps pollinate plants. Some plants have pollen which floats on water. When it reaches another plant of the same type, cross-pollination occurs. Wind is another agent, and many trees, shrubs, and grasses need wind to carry their pollen. Plants that depend on water and wind don't need beautiful, fragrant flowers, but they do need lots of pollen. Water and wind waste pollen. Much of it will float away or blow onto the wrong kinds of plants.

Just as plants depend upon insects, water, and wind to carry pollen, they also need these helpers to carry their seeds. Some seeds travel long distances from their original home. How do they do this? The seeds of some plants have tiny hooks on them, which cling to feathers and fur. People also carry these hooked seeds on their clothing. Some seeds, like thistle and dandelion seeds, are feathery, weighing almost nothing. These can be blown far by winds. Still other seeds are in fruits eaten by birds and carried faraway before being dropped.

Short-tailed beavertail cactus,
an endangered plant

Of course, plant seeds that are carried far by any agent must drop to the ground in a place where the climate and soil are right if their move is to be a permanent one. Many seeds left behind by birds, water, or wind dry up and die. Some, however, find suitable places to grow. In this way, plants of the same kind may be found all over the world.

In modern times, many plants travel because humans travel. People moving to new homes take with them the plants they have depended on for food, shade, or ornament. Again, however, the new climate and soil may keep the foreign plant from growing successfully.

You know that over millions of years animals moved about as the world's climate changed during a series of glaciers and ice ages. What did plants do during these ages? Could they migrate? Plants that lived in places where the climate changed a great deal would ordinarily have died. Some kinds of plants became extinct because of changes in nature. Of course, many more plants have become extinct or are in danger because humans have destroyed their habitats.

Rose

Cherries

E. R. Degginger/Earth Scenes

Larry Lefever from Grant Heilman

Grant Heilman

Bridal wreath

Plant Families

Scientists have divided the plant kingdom into families. Plants that have similar flowers are in the same family. Some of these also have stems or leaves that are similar. For example, members of the mint family have square stems and members of the grass family have long slender leaves.

One large family, the rose family, includes plants that are very small and others that are very large. You may not have realized that cherries and apricots are related to the roses that grow in gardens and parks. In addition, almost all fruit trees, strawberry plants, raspberry bushes, spirea bushes (sometimes called bridal wreath), and the hawthorne are in the rose family. Look carefully sometime at the flowers from these plants and you will see why scientists put all of these in the same group.

The members of the rose family have some parts of their flowers that are arranged in fives. There are usually five sepals covering the buds. If inside the sepals there are more than five petals, they, too, are arranged in groups of five. Sometimes it is hard to see this because the petals grow so closely. Inside rose flowers are several stamens and one or more pistils.

Early in the growing season, a tall healthy plum tree will be bright with fragrant flowers. Bees will visit the blossoms frequently to get the sweet nectar. They carry pollen from one blossom to another. Several pollen grains will catch in the sticky top of each blossom's pistil. Usually, after it has been pollinated, a plum seed begins to grow and the petals of the flower wilt and fall off.

In plum trees, the ovary of the blossom begins to grow as soon as the ovule inside is fertilized. The ovary part of the blossom, in time, becomes the fruit that we eat, and the ovule becomes the seed. As the seed grows, food for the young plant is stored in it.

Before long, the fruit is ripe and ready to eat. The stone inside the ripe plum is a seed; it can grow if it is planted in the right soil and cared for properly.

Plum trees, however, grow very slowly. Modern methods for growing fruit trees may not depend upon the seed. New fruit trees usually are started from branches cut from fruit trees which have especially good fruit.

The rose family is on almost every continent on Earth. Some plant from the family grows in the hottest climates and in all but the very coldest. There are more than 3,000 members of this family.

Another common group of plants is the composite family. A *composite* is a plant with a group of flowers growing so close together that they look like one flower. All the plants in this family have many flowers arranged in tight clusters. The sunflower, daisy, dandelion, and aster are in this group.

Sunflower

Asters

Brian Parker/TOM STACK & ASSOCIATES

The black-eyed Susan belongs to the composite family of flowers. Like other composites, it is made up of many little flowers together on one head. In fact, the black-eyed Susan is made up of two kinds of smaller flowers. All around the outside there is a row of bright yellow petals which hang slightly. The flowers of this outer ring have petals to attract insects but have neither stamens nor pistils. The many little, almost purple-colored flowers growing close together at the center have both stamens and pistils but no petals.

The stamens of the black-eyed Susan produce a bright yellow pollen, but the pistils of the flower are seldom ready to receive pollen when its own pollen is ripe. But the pollen is not wasted. It is carried by bees and other insects to black-eyed Susans whose pistils are ready to be pollinated. In like manner, the first flower will obtain pollen at the time its pistils are ready to be pollinated.

Lettuce

Although the black-eyed Susan is often cultivated for its bright flowers, it is sometimes looked upon as a problem. You remember that animals are sometimes considered pests because they are in the wrong place or because there are too many of them for the habitat. For the same reasons, some plants are considered pests, or *weeds*.

Another composite, the sunflower, is often cultivated for its seeds. These seeds have many uses: food for livestock, oil, birdseed, and snacks for people.

Of all flowering plant families, the composite is the largest. Many of its members are garden flowers such as the daisy, chrysanthemum, zinnia, dahlia, and aster. Others grow wild: goldenrod, dandelion, ragweed, Spanish needle, Canada thistle, and burdock. Some familiar vegetables are members of the composite family. Lettuce, endive, and artichokes are composites.

Look carefully at an onion and a white lily. Can you see anything that tells you these two plants are members of the same family? The lily family is another of the world's large families of plants. About 3,500 different plants belong to this family and they can be found on every continent on Earth, except Antarctica.

People have grown lilies for hundreds of years. Many of them are grown just for their beautiful flowers. Some lilies are cultivated in hothouses and gardens. Others grow wild. The yucca is a member of the lily family. So are the Easter lily, sego lily, tiger lily, hyacinth, and tulip.

Plants in the lily family grow from scaly bulbs that send forth bare or leafy upright stems. The flowers usually have six petals and are bell-shaped. At the base of each petal is a groove that bears nectar.

If you count the stamens in a lily flower, you will find that there are six. There is also a long pistil. Its tip is a three-lobed stigma. While the flowers in the lily family are alike in these and other ways, they may vary greatly in color. The Easter lily is white. Tiger lilies are bright orange with darker spots. Both hyacinths and tulips come in many colors.

Day lilies

Grant Heilman

Some other well-known flowers in this family are the Madonna lily, day lily, wood lily, the leopard lily, which is very tall, and the lily of the valley, which looks like a row of tiny bells on a stalk, has a strong fragance, and often grows wild.

Another wildflower, the dogtooth violet, belongs to the lily family. Its flowers are gold-yellow and it grows in moist woods and swampy places. A small, brilliant red lily may be found growing wild in some of the few remaining natural prairies. Water lilies, despite their name, are not members of the lily family.

The lily family, like the composites, includes vegetables. Asparagus, garlic, leeks, and onions are members of the lily family.

Onions

A grazing bison

Grass—Another Plant with Seeds

For many animals in all parts of the world, domesticated and wild, grass is the most important source of food. Bison, buffalo, horses, deer, zebras, kangaroos, sheep, goats, and pigs eat their way across large grassy areas. Small animals, too, such as rabbits, hares, gophers, prairie dogs, and such insects as grasshoppers and caterpillars depend upon grass for food. Human beings eat grass, too. When we eat cereal or anything made with flour, we are eating grass. Corn, wheat, sugarcane, barley, bamboo, rice, millet, sorghum, and oats are all grasses and are the bases of many common foods.

Like composites and roses, grasses make up one of the world's largest plant families, growing on about 20 percent of Earth's surface.

All plants included in the grass family have flowers and stems which are much alike. Grass flowers, however, don't produce nectar, aren't brightly colored, have no odor, and have no petals. Since grasses are pollinated by the wind, they don't need these things to attract insects.

Corn is one kind of grass. Corn was first grown in North and South America and is still used mostly on those continents. Very long ago, Indians learned to plant, grind, and use this grass for food. There were dozens of types of corn; some grew well in the cool weather of Canada or Chile and some grew in the hot, wet climate of the Amazon. The Incas grew corn on the sides of the Andean mountains, and the Hopis irrigated small parts of the hot, dry desert and grew corn. Not all of these varieties of corn are used today. Most of the corn produced now comes from varieties scientists have developed.

The corn plant produces male and female flowers. The male flowers are on tassels. They grow on the very tops of the corn plants and produce a great deal of pollen. Female flowers are on the cobs, which grow along the sides of the stems. There are many pistils on each cob and each pistil ends in a threadlike fiber that protrudes from the top of the cob. Together, all the fibers are called corn silk.

When pollen on the tassel is ripe, it may fall on the silk of the same plant or it may be carried by the wind to another corn plant. After pollen has reached the silk, it works its way down the long fine fiber of silk in order to reach an ovule and help make a seed, or kernel. Each of the hundreds of kernels on an ear of corn is the result of pollen reaching a fiber of corn silk.

You know that in most cases plants that come from cross-pollination are stronger and better than those that are self-pollinated. Cross-pollinated corn is usually healthier and better able to stand bad weather, and it may also have larger and better-shaped ears. Corn today doesn't usually grow wild; it is grown by farmers.

The farmers often give the corn special care to make sure that it is cross-pollinated and it produces the best possible seeds for planting in the next growing season. Two carefully selected kinds of corn are planted in alternate rows throughout the field. Just before pollination, the tassels in all the rows containing one kind of corn are clipped off. Then the silk of these corn plants can't receive any pollen from tassels of their own plants but only the pollen which comes from the tassels of the other kind in the adjoining rows. In this way it is certain that half of the field—that is, the kind of corn from which the tassels have been removed—will be cross-pollinated. The corn which grows on these plants is called *hybrid* corn. Most farmers today use only hybrid corn for seed.

The outsides of the stems, or stalks, of corn plants are exceptionally strong, and when the corn gets ripe, the stalks are very stiff and hard to break. The leaves are long, wavy, and narrow, with tough veins. If the leaves were wider or didn't have veins, they would be torn more

Grant Heilman

easily by the wind. Where the ends of the leaves are attached to the stalks, they are fastened all the way around the stalks. Although corn is bigger than other cereal plants, all are much alike in other ways. The stems of grasses are jointed, hard on the outside, and soft or hollow on the inside.

Cereal grasses are the chief source of food for human beings all over the world. Do you know why these grasses are so important to our health? You remember that some plants store food in the seeds they produce. Grasses turn this food into protein and carbohydrates, and people need these two kinds of foods. Grasses also furnish food for the animals that supply eggs, milk, and meat.

Some grasses are used in other ways. Sugarcane is processed to make sugar and syrup. Syrup is also made from corn. Bamboo, the largest of the grasses, is used for food and also to build shelters and make furniture. Other grasses are used to create beautiful lawns and gardens. Taller grasses are planted for decoration. Grass-covered fields are required for many sports.

Grasses grow on about one-fifth of Earth's surface. In different climates, of course, different kinds of grass will survive best. Broad, open fields dominated by grasses have been given different names, depending on the climate and the kinds of grass. *Savannas* are grasslands in warm climates that have an extremely dry season followed by a wet season. Grass in the savanna is often over three feet (1 m) high. *Temperate grasslands* are usually in the middle sections of large continents where there are cold winters and hot summers. These kinds of grasslands are found in North America, South America, Europe, Asia, and southern Africa. Some of the prairie grasses growing in these places may be over 6½ feet (2 m) high while the shorter grasses will be less than two feet (0.6 m). Another wide expanse of grass can be found in the *tundra*. A tundra is a cold desert, near the Arctic. Grasses on the tundra usually grow in clumps called *tussocks*. All over Earth, grasses are growing—in yards and fields, and even between the cracks in city pavement. It is easy to see that grass is an important and hardy plant.

Vegetable garden

Plants for Food

You know that some plants in the rose family bear fruits that we consider good food—strawberries, apples, plums, and peaches, for example. Some plant parts in other families are also edible. We call these foods vegetables.

At the beginning of a growing season, a gardener will turn over the soil in the vegetable plot where new plants will be placed or where seeds are to be sown. Some vegetables, called *perennials*, won't have to be replanted. The word *perennial* means "by the year." The roots of these plants live in the soil during the cool season and the plants will come up every year. Plants called *annuals* live one year, produce seeds, and die. *Biennials* produce a large root the first year and then come up the next spring to produce seeds.

Some annuals and biennials are planted from seed. Others are bulbs. Still others have been started indoors and the tiny plants must be moved, or *transplanted*.

Vegetables are an important part of the foods we eat and we eat different parts of different kinds of vegetables. These vegetables manufacture their food and store it in a part of the plant. We use that part for food. Each part of a plant is made of millions of tiny cells and each part serves a purpose. For example, root cells absorb water and minerals from the soil. But the most wonderful process, the manufacture of sugar for plant growth, takes place in the cells of the green leaves. The green chlorophyll acts on the water and the carbon dioxide from the air to produce food. You know that this process is called photosynthesis.

After sugar is formed in the leaves, most plants change some of it to another kind of food before they store it away. For example, the potato plant changes much of the sugar to starch before storing it in the underground stem. Peas and beans form proteins from much of their sugar and store the protein in the seeds. The main food value of a green garden plant may be in the roots, stems, buds, leaves, flowers, seeds, or fruits. Since each plant manufactures a different kind of food, we can have a balanced diet if we eat a variety of plant parts from many different vegetables.

We eat the roots of radishes, carrots, cassava, and turnips. Celery and rhubarb are stems. Cauliflower and broccoli are stalks and flowers. Beans, peas, peanuts, and corn (or any other grain) are seeds. Pumpkins, melons, and tomatoes are fruits.

Oak

Spruce

Trees

Some of the largest seed-producing plants are trees. There are thousands of kinds of trees and they grow on all continents, with the exception of Antarctica, and on most islands. Trees are woody plants, with trunks, branches, and leaves or needles. Most trees also bear flowers, but many have cones instead. A tree's flowers or cones hold the seeds produced by the tree.

All trees must drop old leaves and needles and grow new ones. Trees that drop all of their leaves in one season are called *deciduous* trees. Trees that lose their leaves a few at a time and are never bare are called *evergreens*.

One of the best-known kinds of deciduous trees is the oak and its relative, the beech tree. Both grow best in climates that have cold winters and warm summers. They can be found across Europe, Asia, and North America. Oak trees are often grown for their wood. Many kinds of furniture are made of oak. One type of oak that is grown in Portugal is also valuable because its bark can be stripped every nine or ten years and the cork layer used to make all kinds of products.

The elm is another well-known deciduous tree. Elms grow on some part of every continent except Antarctica. They are often grown as shade trees.

There are also many kinds of evergreen trees and these grow all over the world. Among the best-known are firs, spruces, hemlocks, and pines.

Many evergreens bear cones, rather than flowers. The needles of these trees are quite different from one another. Some have short needles, some have long ones. Spruce needles are four-sided and sharp on the points. Fir trees have flat, blunt needles. The needles of the cedar are wide and not sharp. Hemlock, another evergreen, also has flat, blunt needles.

A white pine is an evergreen. Early in its growing season, clusters of short reddish-brown tufts, or *catkins*, appear near the tips of some of the twigs of the tree. There are several of these catkins in each cluster and they produce pollen. On the tips, or near the tips, of many other branches, tiny pinkish-green cones appear. They point up in the air and, like the pistils of flowers, receive the pollen. The cones are made up of many small scales, and at the base of each scale there are two ovules.

During the warm days early in the season, the pollen ripens and is picked up by the wind. It is carried easily because each little grain has two wings. In the meantime, the cones open and spread their scales to form little shovels. So much pollen from the catkins is given off into the air that some of it is sure to be carried down behind the many scales of the cones. After the cones are pollinated, the scales close back against them; then the cones slowly turn downward.

Behind the cone scales, pollen tubes grow into the ovules. Two seeds begin to form behind each scale. When the pine cone is about two years old, the scales open and the seeds fall out. Each little winged seed is carried away by the wind. Some seeds reach fertile soil and some grow into new pine trees.

Redwoods

Trees come in many sizes. Some of the biggest trees in North America are sequoia trees and they grow to be five times as tall as most shade trees—over 300 feet (90 m). They may be as much as 30 feet (9 m) thick at the base. These trees were named for a famous Cherokee Indian, Sequoya, who invented a system of writing for the Cherokee language.

There are two kinds of huge trees, the sequoias and the redwoods. The redwoods are the taller of the two and the sequoias are thicker around. Some of these trees have been standing for more than 3,000 years. The redwoods are native only along the foggy coastal regions of northern California and Oregon. The sequoias grow inland in central California on the western slopes of the Sierra Nevadas. Both trees are evergreens and bear cones.

A large area of trees is called a forest. There are no forests of sequoias left anywhere. When people began to settle in California, the trees were cut down to make way for homes and farms. Redwoods were cut to produce the beautiful redwood lumber that is used for

Firs killed by acid rain

decks and furniture. Now some of the remaining groves of trees are protected by the government and are part of the United States National Forests.

Cutting down entire forests is called *deforestation*. Deforestation is a very serious problem in many parts of the world. The Himalayan mountains and the Amazon forests are two places in which trees are being cut so rapidly that the forests may be completely gone in the near future. Another problem for forests is *acid rain*. Some scientists think that acid rain is causing damage in more than 17 million acres (6,880,000 hectares) of forest in about 20 countries. Acid rain is caused by rain falling through air filled with dangerous chemicals given off by the burning of oil, gas, and coal. The rain picks up the chemicals and the chemicals destroy the trees. Many scientists and other people all over the world are working on ways to save the forests that are left.

Plants without Seeds

The biggest plants in all the oceans of the world are the giant kelps. These huge plants sometimes grow to a length of 150 feet (45 m). They don't stand up straight and tall like trees. They look more like vines.

These strange plants don't have roots like land plants. Instead they have *holdfasts*, which anchor the plants to the shallow bottom of the ocean along rocky shores.

Giant kelps don't have real leaves either. They do, however, have organs that look something like leaves that may be a yard (0.9 m) long and 10 inches (25 cm) wide. A small air bladder at the base of each leaflike organ acts as a float and helps keep parts of the kelp near the top of the water where they can get sunlight. Like other green plants, kelps need light with which to manufacture their food.

These plants live many years. New plants grow from the holdfasts. Kelp plants reproduce by means of spores instead of seeds.

Giant kelp is often called seaweed. Seaweed can be used in many ways. People may eat it; it is often used as fertilizer; it is used as food for farm animals. Some useful products can be made from seaweed. Among these is agar, a substance used in candy and other foods.

Another plant without seeds is the fern. During the Coal Age, many thousands of years ago, immense forests of ferns as tall as trees grew throughout the world. Much smaller ferns grow in many parts of the world today.

When ferns first come through the ground, each leafy branch, or frond, forms a small ball which unrolls as it grows. When partly open, a frond is shaped much like the head of a violin. Young ferns are often called fiddle heads for this reason.

Ferns have no flowers and no seeds. Instead, many ferns have little cases that look like small brown dots on the underside of the leaves. These cases contain many tiny spores. Although a fern spore is but one cell and is so small that it can be seen only under a microscope, it serves the fern in much the same way as a seed serves a plant. When the spore cases are ripe, they spring open with such force that the spores are thrown into the air. The wind then carries them. The spores that fall in places where the soil and temperature are right and where there is plenty of moisture will live and grow.

Each spore grows into a little flat green body about the size of a thumbnail and shaped somewhat like a heart. It clings to the ground by hairlike roots. This body is called a *prothallium* which means "before the shoot." Two types of bumps grow on the underside of the prothallium. Although these bumps don't have stamens and pistils, they do for the prothallium what stamens and pistils do for flowers. When the bumps are ripe, the male cells of the one type travel forth in moisture in all directions. When one of these cells reaches the second kind of bump, it unites with a female cell of that particular bump and a fern begins to grow. The new plant grows slowly and it may take several years to develop into a full-sized fern.

Wild ferns usually grow in deep woods where it is shady and damp. There are many kinds of ferns. Because the spores are so easily spread by the wind, ferns may be found just about anywhere. The most widespread fern is probably the brittle bladder fern. Other well-known types of ferns are the lacy maidenhair fern, the royal fern, and the bead fern.

FUNGI

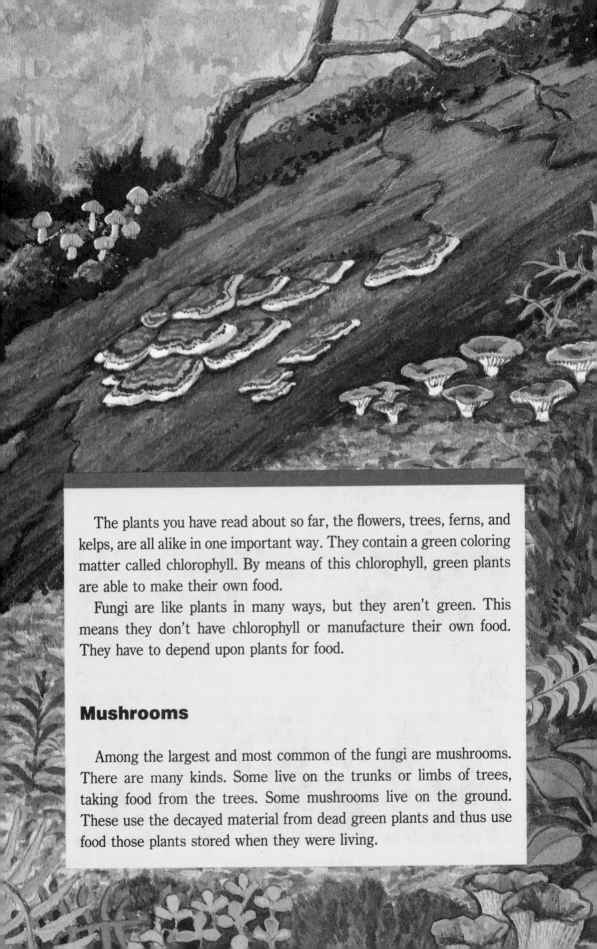

The plants you have read about so far, the flowers, trees, ferns, and kelps, are all alike in one important way. They contain a green coloring matter called chlorophyll. By means of this chlorophyll, green plants are able to make their own food.

Fungi are like plants in many ways, but they aren't green. This means they don't have chlorophyll or manufacture their own food. They have to depend upon plants for food.

Mushrooms

Among the largest and most common of the fungi are mushrooms. There are many kinds. Some live on the trunks or limbs of trees, taking food from the trees. Some mushrooms live on the ground. These use the decayed material from dead green plants and thus use food those plants stored when they were living.

Like ferns and kelps, mushrooms have tiny spores instead of seeds. If you shake a mushroom, a cloud of what appears to be dust comes from it. This isn't dust; it is millions of tiny spores. Each mushroom contains a large number of spores. Most of them will be lost as they blow about. Only those that land in suitable places will grow. Mushrooms grow best in warm, moist places and most kinds need shade.

Parasol mushrooms are common. When a spore from this mushroom is carried by the wind to some rich, moist soil, the spore takes in a great deal of water and starts to swell. Soon a fine white thread begins to grow from the side. The little thread takes food from decaying plants. It grows fast, branching again and again until a network of rootlike threads has formed. This network of threads is called the *mycelium*.

Next, a tiny knob, or button, begins to grow on the side of one thread. On a day when the weather is very warm, the button pushes up through the surface of the ground, growing very quickly. The button breaks around the top of the stem and the cap rises on the stem. No longer a button but a raised white parasol, the mushroom keeps growing until its cap is perhaps five inches (13 cm) wide and its stem about nine inches (23 cm) tall.

Parasol mushrooms

Oyster mushrooms

Under the cap of the mushroom there are many folds which hang down like white curtains, close to one another. These are called *gills* and tiny white spores grow on the sides of them. When the spores are ripe, some will drop to the ground and others will be carried away by wind.

After the spores ripen and leave, the parasol part of the plant dies, but the threadlike roots under the ground continue to live. New little bumps are formed and on the first warm, moist day, other mushrooms are almost sure to appear.

Many other types of mushrooms are shaped like umbrellas. Most of them have gills and form spores in the same way, but not all of the spores are white like those of the parasol mushroom. The orange-milk mushroom has yellowish-brown spores, the meadow mushroom has pink ones, and the inky-cap has black ones.

Oyster mushrooms have gills and white spores but don't have the umbrella shape. They grow so close to one another that they look like one oyster on top of another. Often they have no stems but grow against a tree. If they have stems, the stems are on the side of the cap.

Many mushrooms are edible. People may search for orange-milk mushrooms, meadow mushrooms, inky-caps, parasol mushrooms, and oyster mushrooms to use for food. A morel mushroom is one of the most prized and best-tasting of mushrooms. It has a cap shaped somewhat like a sponge. The morel has no gills and the spores grow in tiny sacs in the cap. This mushroom may grow to be as tall as four inches (10 cm).

One of the most beautiful mushrooms is the sulphur mushroom, which grows on the trunks of trees. It is sometimes called a shelf fungus because it grows out from the side of the tree like a small shelf. It doesn't have gills or sacs, but it has little pores in which the spores grow. This mushroom is a bright yellow color, like the sulphur for which it is named.

A tree that has sulphur mushrooms growing on it is almost sure to die because the mushrooms' threadlike roots steal so much of its food. The mushrooms that grow on trees may also cause trouble for the tree by opening up its bark so that insects can attack the tree more easily.

Another common mushroom, often found in pastures, is called a puff ball. Some puff balls grow larger than basketballs; others remain as small as marbles. If these mushrooms are gathered when they are young, they are good to eat, but when they are ripe and full of dustlike spores, they are inedible.

Another mushroom is shaped like a star. Like the puff ball, the earth star mushroom is full of spores when it is ripe. They come out through a little hole at the top. The earth star's points curl back or down when the weather is dry, but the points straighten out when wet weather comes. Most earth stars aren't more than two or three inches (5-8 cm) across when the points are stretched out flat.

Mushrooms help dead leaves and twigs decay so they can add nutrients to the soil. Also, many mushrooms are edible, nourishing, and easy to prepare. But mushrooms should NEVER be gathered by anyone who doesn't know a great deal about them. Certain kinds of mushrooms are very poisonous. Unfortunately, the poisonous kind may look like some of the edible ones. For example, one kind of amanita that is extremely poisonous and deadly looks very much like another amanita that is safe to eat.

Mold

Another fungus we see everywhere is mold. Mold doesn't need soil or sunshine or even much water, although it must have some moisture. If you would like to experiment with growing mold, put a piece of bread or fruit in a warm place out of the sunlight. Cover it to keep the food moist and watch the mold grow. You don't even have to plant mold. It has already been planted when spores in the air came in contact with the food.

Like mushrooms, small mold spores send out threads which branch and form a network of threads called a mycelium. When the threads are ready to produce spores, they send up stems so tiny that many of them together look almost like fur. The spores are produced on or near the ends of these stems.

Some kinds of mold produce spores in small round cases at the ends of the stems. The spore cases may be black, blue, yellow, or green.

There are many kinds of molds and they grow on almost everything which comes from plants and animals. They grow on leather and cloth as well as on food.

Some kinds of mold are used to help make food for us. Several kinds of cheese get their special flavors because of the mold which has been added to them. If you have seen a creamy white cheese with bluish streaks through it, you may be sure the streaks are mold. Another blue mold is important in making a drug called penicillin.

There is a class of molds, called slime molds, that are valuable because they cause dead plants to decay and make the soil richer. If you ever see a log on the ground, remove some of the loose bark. You will probably see the red, blue, yellow, or brown patches that are the spores of a slime mold.

Like mushrooms, molds can be either helpful or harmful to people. Because we know that mold won't grow in moving air or in places that are light, dry, or cold, we can find ways to keep molds from growing in places where we don't want them and we can help them to grow where we do want them.

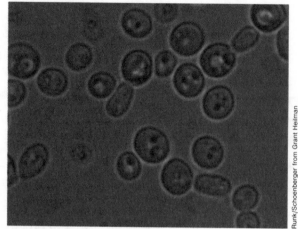

Yeast cells

Runk/Schoenberger from Grant Heilman

Yeast

There is a third kind of fungus which affects us every day. It is called *yeast*. Long ago people ate bread that was heavy and solid. Then it was discovered that dough a day or two old would puff up if it was left standing in a warm place. Bread baked from this dough was full of little holes, making it lighter and easier to eat. If the microscope had been invented then, bakers would have seen a tiny one-celled fungus in the dough. This fungus, yeast, depends on sugar for its food. If the temperature is warm and there is sugar and water, yeast, which is everywhere in the air, will grow and produce more cells like itself. Yeast grows by forming little bumps on the sides of a cell. These bumps, or buds, get larger and form little buds of their own. Sometimes the buds hang together like a string of beads, but they usually fall apart and start new strings.

Like all other living things, yeast uses food and throws off materials it doesn't need. The yeast needs sugar and throws off carbon dioxide gas and alcohol. Carbon dioxide is the gas that green plants need to make food, but since the yeast doesn't make its own food, it gets rid of the carbon dioxide.

Bread dough is almost all flour, water, sugar, and salt. It is thick and tough and stretches when it is pulled. The carbon dioxide given off by yeast that is in bread dough can't get out. The dough just stretches when the gas tries to escape, and soon there are little pockets of gas all through the dough. Since the gas has stretched the dough, it takes up more space than it did. We say that the dough "rises." When the bread is baked, the yeast is killed. The alcohol evaporates and the carbon dioxide escapes. The finished bread is light because of the small holes left by the alcohol and gas.

Long ago people used pieces of old dough to start new loaves of bread. Today packages of yeast are used for baking. This yeast may be dry and powdery or in moist cakes. It won't grow as long as it is sealed tightly and kept cold.

Yeast also gets into fruit juices that have been left open to the air. Yeast uses up the sugar, making the fruit juice sour. The carbon dioxide gas can get out of the liquid, but the alcohol remains. This is a part of the process by which wine and other alcoholic drinks are made.

This working of yeast in a food is called *fermentation*. One reason for canning food is to keep it from fermenting. Food that is to be canned is first heated to kill the yeast and any molds or bacteria. Then it is sealed to keep the air away.

Although yeast fungi have only one cell and are so tiny they can be seen only through a microscope, they are a very important part of some foods and they are also capable of doing damage.

Yeast breads

Monerans and Protists

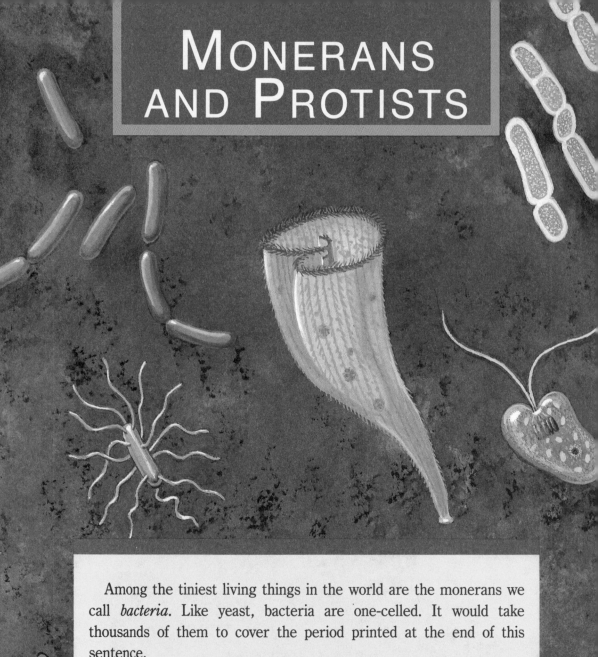

Among the tiniest living things in the world are the monerans we call *bacteria*. Like yeast, bacteria are one-celled. It would take thousands of them to cover the period printed at the end of this sentence.

Until microscopes were invented, no one suspected the existence of bacteria. The first person to see bacteria thought they were animals and called them "little beasties." Later they were thought to be plants. Most scientists today consider bacteria to be in a separate kingdom.

Bacteria may be small, but they can reproduce themselves faster than any other known body. In some cases, it takes only 20 minutes for a single bacterium to become two.

A bacterium takes in food and water, and soon a double wall grows through the center of the cell. The double wall then divides, leaving

two cells instead of one. Each of the new cells may divide again in another 20 minutes. By the end of four hours, if they continue to multiply at this rate, and if all of the bacteria live, there could be over 4,000 bacteria instead of one.

As seen through a microscope, most bacteria are round, rod-shaped, or curly. There are many kinds of bacteria. Bacteria can be found everywhere—in air, water, soil, on our hands, in our bodies. Many kinds are helpful to animals and plants; others cause serious diseases.

Helpful bacteria cause the decay of dead plants and animals. If they didn't do this important work, the world would soon be piled high with dead things. When bacteria cause waste materials to decay, valuable substances are returned to the soil to enrich it.

Some bacteria help us to make certain kinds of foods, such as cheese and butter. Other kinds of bacteria help us to digest the food we eat.

Another kind of helpful bacteria, called nitrogen-fixing bacteria, live in little bumps on the roots of certain plants, such as clover. As they grow, these bacteria take nitrogen gas from the air and put it into the soil in a form which plants can use. Green plants need nitrogen compounds in order to grow and the only way they can take it in is from the soil.

Harmful bacteria are often called germs. Many of them don't cause us much trouble when rules of cleanliness are followed. Scientists and doctors know enough about many bacteria so that we can protect ourselves against them or cure the diseases those bacteria cause.

One way we protect ourselves from harmful bacteria is by keeping most foods cool in refrigerators. Bacteria can't grow well in the cold. If food is heated enough, most bacteria will be killed. Then by sealing the food so no more bacteria can get in, we can keep the food safely. Also, drying some foods is a good way to preserve them because most bacteria can't grow where it is dry.

In general, these tiny monerans are more helpful than harmful and we wouldn't be able to live without them.

Like monerans, protists are organisms that can't be easily classified as plants or animals. When the protista kingdom was originally proposed, it included all single-celled organisms and organisms with no cells. Now most scientists classify bacteria and blue-green algae as monerans. Protists are one-celled organisms that have well defined cell nuclei; they include protozoa, some algae, and certain fungi.

Protozoa

ECOLOGY

The earlier chapters in this book are about groups of living things. But if you look around, you will discover that no one group ever lives by itself. There is a simple reason for this. Plants, animals, fungi, monerans, and protists depend upon each other. The study of how living things depend on each other and on their environment is called *ecology.*

Do you know why every living thing depends on plants? Most green plants can make their own food, for all they need is sunlight, air, water, and soil that is filled with minerals. Other living things eat food that comes directly or indirectly from green plants.

Plants also provide shelter for animals. Many birds build nests in trees. Deer and other animals use brush for shelter. Beavers cut down trees to build lodges. People use plants for shelter, too—many of our homes are built of wood.

How do animals help plants? You know that bees and other insects, as well as birds and some larger animals, help pollinate plants. Animals also help by scattering plant seeds.

Alan Pitcairn from Grant Heilman

Even after they are dead, plants and animals help one another. When plants die, they decay. Animals decay, too. Rain and snow help this decayed matter sink into the soil. Smaller living things—protists, fungi, and monerans—help with this process of decay. This process enriches the soil by adding chemicals to it. Green plants grow from the soil, fungi and animals live on the green plants, and the *cycle,* or pattern, begins again.

Plants and animals help each other in another important way. Each gives off waste matter the other can use. When they breathe, animals take oxygen from the air and give off carbon dioxide. Plants take the carbon dioxide from the air and use it in making food. They return oxygen to the air. Animals breathe in the oxygen. Again you see the cycle in action. Plants and animals help one another to survive.

You can see that all living things depend upon one another. However, all kinds of plants and animals don't live in the same place. For example, elephants and polar bears don't share a territory. The place each plant and animal lives is determined by the climate it needs to survive. The community of living things in any climate is called a *biome.* Every biome has a regular population of certain kinds of plants and animals.

The creatures in any biome depend upon each other, and nature tries to keep a balance between them. Each year some plants and animals die because they are weak. The strong ones survive. All plants and animals have enemies. Insects eat plants; birds eat insects. The cycle goes on and on.

186   *Plant and Animal Ways*

Grant Heilman

Weather also keeps the balance between plants and animals. For example, if there is too much rain, it washes away the soil and plants can't grow. If the plants aren't available, some animals will have no food. As long as living things exist, nature will help keep a balance between them.

Often, however, people interfere with the balance of nature. They plant crops and root up native plants. How does this affect the animals? People sometimes kill animals that are annoying to them. How does this affect the plants?

When you see the word *biome*, it usually means a large area, like the Amazon rain forest, but in some ways, your farm or your back yard is a biome. Certain kinds of weeds, flowers, grasses, fungi, and small animals live there. What lives there depends partly on where you live on Earth, and partly on how you care for your land. You can add water or you can see what grows without extra water. You can let native plants grow or you can plant things that aren't native to your part of the world. You can control the biome that is your farm or yard.

In the same way, people sometimes try to control the larger biomes all over the world. Do you think we should do that? Would Earth be a better place if we let each biome grow naturally? Would it be a better place if we controlled the biomes more than we do?

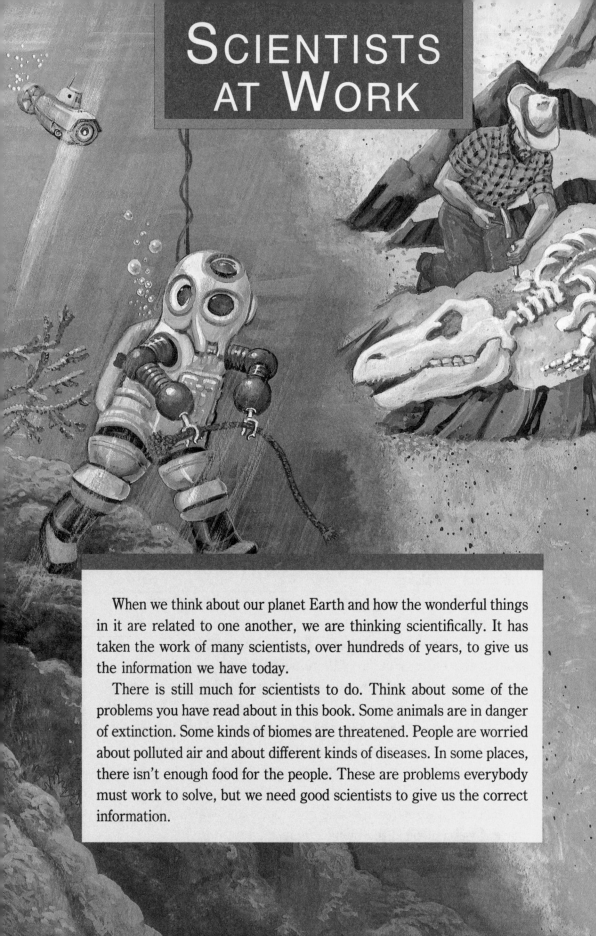

SCIENTISTS AT WORK

When we think about our planet Earth and how the wonderful things in it are related to one another, we are thinking scientifically. It has taken the work of many scientists, over hundreds of years, to give us the information we have today.

There is still much for scientists to do. Think about some of the problems you have read about in this book. Some animals are in danger of extinction. Some kinds of biomes are threatened. People are worried about polluted air and about different kinds of diseases. In some places, there isn't enough food for the people. These are problems everybody must work to solve, but we need good scientists to give us the correct information.

Many scientists do most of their work in *research*. This means they study and then write about what they have discovered. Many research scientists work in laboratories, using microscopes, computers, and other equipment to learn more about the universe. Other research scientists have gone into space with astronauts to carry out experiments. Still others have gone to the bottom of the great oceans or spent years in forests or deserts studying the living and nonliving things they find there.

Still other scientists spend most of their time using, or *applying*, the information gained by research. These men and women are teachers, inventors, and technicians. They do many, many things every day to make our Earth safer and to make our lives better.

What do you think you have to be like to be a scientist? Do you know anybody who might be a good scientist? What about you?

Index

eyes: compound, 119, 130, 136; simple, 119, 130

F

families: animals, 17; plant, 156
fermentation, 181
ferns, 147, 148, 173
fins, 46, 103
fish, 14, 100-107; diagram, 103; goldfish, 102-103; king salmon, 104-107
Fishes, Age of, 14
fish ladders, 106
flicker, 70
flies: see houseflies
flower: diagrams, 148, 149
flowering plants, 148-171
fossils, 14, 18
fox, 25
frogs, 95-99
fungi, 8, 9, 146, 174-181

G

garden spider, 140-141
geese, 61, 64, 66
geranium, 151
germs, 184
giant tortoise, 88
gills, 14, 95, 96, 97, 101, 102, 110, 112-113, 177
golden plover, 65
goldfish, 102-103
gorilla, 31, 32
grasses, 162-165
grasshoppers, 129-131
green plants, 145-147, 167, 184, 185-186
green turtle, 89
grubs, 125-126
guide dog, 27

H

habitat, 57
hares, 38-39
herbivorous animal, 42
hibernation, 86; frog, 97; snake, 86; turtle, 89
hive: see beehive
holdfasts, 172
Holland Lop (rabbit), 39
honey, 126, 127, 128
honeybee, 125-128
honeycomb, 125-128
hooved animals, 17-24
horses, 18-24; diagram, 18
houseflies, 135-137

hummingbird, 76-77
humpback whale, 47-48
hyena, 30

I

inky-cap mushroom, 177, 178
insectivores, 40
insects, 12, 119-137, 139; ant, 120-123; bee, 123-128; butterfly, 132-134; fly, 135-137; grasshopper, 129-131; mosquito, 135-137; moth, 134
invertebrates, 11-12, 108-143
ivory-billed woodpecker, 71-72

K

kangaroo, 50
katydid, 130
kelps, 172-173
kingdoms, 8-9
king salmon, 104-107
kiwi, 75
koala, 50

L

land snail, 117
larvae: ant, 121; bee, 124, 125; butterfly, 133; fly, 136; mosquito, 136; moth, 134, 153
leaf-cutting ant, 123
leopard, 29, 30
leopard frog, 99
lettuce, 159
lily family, 160-161
lion, 29-30
living things, 7-9, 14
locust, 130, 131
long-horned grasshopper, 130-131

M

mammals, 14, 16-57; ape, 31, 32; bat, 41; beaver, 35-37; cats, 29-30; dogs, 25-28; dolphin, 49; elephant, 42-44; hare, 38-39; horse, 18-24; lion, 29-30; marsupials, 50; mole, 40; monkeys, 31-32; platypus, 51; rabbit, 38-39; squirrel, 34; whale, 45-48
Mammals, Age of, 14
manatee, 51
marmoset, 31, 32
marsupials, 50
meadow grasshopper: see long-horned grasshopper
meadow mushroom, 177, 178

migration: bird, 61-66, 71, 77; butterfly, 133; fish, 104-107; grasshopper, 131; turtle, 89; whale, 48
mold, 9, 179
mole, 40
monarch butterfly, 132-133
monerans, 8, 9, 182-184
monkeys, 31-32
morel mushroom, 178
Morgan (horse), 23-24
mosquitoes, 135-137
moths, 132, 134, 151, 152
mouse, 33
mule, 24
mushrooms, 9, 175-178
mustang, 21
mycelium, 176, 179

N

nectar, 76, 77, 126, 127, 133
nest: alligator, 91; ant, 120-123; arctic tern, 65; crocodile, 91; hummingbird, 77; mole, 40; ostrich, 74; robin, 68; salmon, 107; squirrel, 34; woodpecker, 71
night crawlers: see earthworms
nonliving things, 7
nymphs, grasshopper, 131

O

oak, 168-169
onion, 160, 161
opossum, 50
orange-milk mushroom, 177, 178
Oriental white stork, 79
ostrich, 73-75
ovary, 149, 153, 157
ovule, 149, 150, 153, 157, 163, 169
oyster, 12, 109-111
oyster mushroom, 177, 178

P

panda, 25, 28
parasol ant, 123
parasol mushroom, 176-177
pearl oyster, 111
penguin, 60
penicillin, 179
perennials, 166
periwinkle, 117
pests, 33, 38, 56, 69, 123, 135, 159
photosynthesis, 145, 167

pileated woodpecker, 71
pinto (horse), 24
pistil, 149, 150, 151, 152, 153,
  157, 158, 160, 163
plant kingdom, 8, 145, 146, 147
plants, 144-173; families, 156-
  161; flowering, 148-171;
  with seeds, 148-171; without
  seeds, 172-173
platypus, 51
plum, 157
poachers, 57
poisonous mushrooms, 178
poisonous snakes, 83, 84-85
poisonous spiders, 140, 141
pollen, 125, 126, 127, 149,
  150, 151, 152, 154, 157,
  158, 169
pollination, 133, 135, 153
pony, 24
prehistoric animals, 14-15, 52-
  57, 93
primates, 31-32
protective coloration: arctic
  tern, 64; butterfly, 132-133;
  frog, 99; ostrich, 74; penguin, 60; rabbit, 39; robin,
  68; snake, 86; turtle, 88;
  zebra, 24
prothallium, 173
protists, 8, 9, 182-184
protozoa, 184
puff ball mushroom, 178
pupa: ant, 121, 123, 124, 126;
  butterfly, 133; fly, 136; mosquito, 136; moth, 134
python, 83

Q
quarter horse, 22
queen ant, 121, 122
queen bee, 124-128
queen conch, 117

R
rabbits, 38-39
raccoon, 25, 28
ratites, 73-75
rats, 33-34
rattlesnake, 85, 86
redheaded woodpecker, 70, 71
redwood tree, 170-171
reproduction: see buds, eggs,
  seeds, spores
reptiles, 14, 80-93; alligator,
  90-92; crocodile, 90-92;
  snake, 82-86; turtle, 87-89

Reptiles, Age of, 14, 147
research, 189
rhea, 75
rhesus monkey, 32
robin, 67-69
rodents, 33-37; beaver, 35-37;
  rat, 33-34; squirrel, 34
rose family, 156-157
ruby-throated hummingbird, 76
ruminants, 17

S
salamander, 99
salmon, 104-107
sandhill crane, 66
sapsucker, 71
scales: alligator, 91; butterfly,
  132; crocodile, 91; fish, 103;
  moth, 134; pine cone, 169;
  snake, 81, 82; turtle, 87
scale wings, 132
sea urchin, 113
seaweed: see kelps
seeds, 148, 150, 153, 154,
  155, 157, 159, 167, 168,
  169
sepals, 149, 157
sequoia, 170-171
shearwater, 65
shells: oyster, 12, 109-110,
  111; snail, 12, 116, 117;
  turtle, 87
Shetland pony, 24
short-horned grasshopper, 130-
  131
silk, corn, 163
silkworm, 134
simple eye, 119, 130
skeleton, 12
skunk, 25, 28
slime molds, 179
snails, 12, 116-117
snakes, 82-86
snapping turtle, 88-89
social insects, 120-128
soldier ant, 123
spawning, 107
sperm whale, 47
spiders, 12, 139-141
sponges, 114-115
spores, 172, 173, 176, 177,
  178, 179
squirrel monkey, 32
squirrels, 34
stamens, 149, 151, 153, 157,
  158, 160
starfish, 110, 112-113

stigma, 149, 150, 153, 160
sulphur mushroom, 178
sunflower, 157, 158, 159

T
tadpoles, 95, 96, 98, 99
tadpole snail, 116
tarantula, 141
Tennessee Walking Horse, 23
termites, 123
terrapin, 87
Thoroughbred (horse), 23
thrush, 67
tiger, 29, 30
toads, 97-99
tortoise, 87
trapdoor spider, 141
tree frogs, 99
trees, 168-171; deciduous,
  168-169; evergreen, 168,
  169; oak, 168-169; plum,
  167; redwood, 170-171;
  sequoia, 170-171; white
  pine, 169
turtles, 87-89
Tyrannosaurus, 15

V
vegetables, 166-167
vertebrates, 11-12, 13-15, 59
vulture, 60

W
warm-blooded animals, 13, 14
wasp, 128, 141
water moccasin, 85
web, 140-141
whales, 45-48
white pine, 169
whooping crane, 66
wolf, 25, 26
woodpeckers, 70-72
worker ant, 121, 122
worker bee, 124-128
worms: see earthworms

Y
yeast, 180-181
yucca moth, 153
yucca plant, 153, 160

Z
zebra, 18, 24